GIRLS JUST WANT
TO HAVE LIKES

GIRLS JUST WANT TO HAVE LIKES

How to Raise Confident Girls in the Face of Social Media Madness

LAURIE WOLK

NEW YORK

NASHVILLE • MELBOURNE • VANCOUVER

GIRLS JUST WANT TO HAVE LIKES

How to Raise Confident Girls in the Face of Social Media Madness

17/18 Ing

17-18

© 2017 Laurie Wolk

DISCARDED

Published in New York, New York, by Morgan James Publishing in partnership with Difference Press. Morgan James is a trademark of Morgan James, LLC. www.MorganJamesPublishing.com

The Morgan James Speakers Group can bring authors to your live event. For more information or to book an event visit The Morgan James Speakers Group at www.TheMorganJamesSpeakersGroup.com.

ISBN 9781683502951 paperback
ISBN 9781683502975 ebook
ISBN 9781683502968 Hardcover
Library of Congress Control Number: 2016917108

Cover Design by:
Galen Hermelle

Interior Design by:
Chris Treccani
www.3dogdesign.net

In an effort to support local communities, raise awareness and funds, Morgan James Publishing donates a percentage of all book sales for the life of each book to Habitat for Humanity Peninsula and Greater Williamsburg.

Get involved today! Visit
www.MorganJamesBuilds.com

DISCLAIMER

Cover Design: Galen Hermelle

Editing: Kate Makled

Author's photo courtesy of Chad David Kraus
Illustrations courtesy of Galen Hermelle, graphic designer; and Ellie Garcia, illustrator

DEDICATION

Bulah
Who knew what would come from a simple
slice of chocolate cake.
Every girl should be so lucky.

J, R and S
My teachers, my comedy relief, my loves.
Every mom should be so blessed.

Mom
Unconditional love, an open heart and lots of listening.
Every daughter should feel so loved.

TABLE OF CONTENTS

AUTHORS NOTE

Hello dear readers!

Before you jump in to read Girls Just Want to Have Likes, I want to be sure that you understand that this book is NOT just for girls. Many of (and by many I mean mostly all) the principles, ideas, exercises and statistics apply to boys as well. In fact, after the eBook hit #1 on Amazon I received countless messages from my readers who had sons that this book really spoke to them for their boys as well. So let's just say between you and I ...

Kids These Days Just Want to Have Likes ...

Enjoy and Happy Reading!

INTRODUCTION

Well, here we are, you and I. Strong, confident, capable parents who want so much for our daughters – yet we feel helpless that we have lost the power to make our dreams for our girls come true.

Social media channels and all the other connected screens in our homes, seem to have taken that power from us.

These days, our girls seem to care more about their smart phones and getting "likes" than they do about us, or perhaps anything else.

* * *

From the day I was told "It's a girl," I dreamed about sharing everything with her. Especially the secrets of "girlhood" that I had learned the hard way in my youth. I bet you feel the same.

I told myself I was going to build a "better" me because of her, and that with unconditional love, strong values and my hard won life experiences, my daughter would in turn grow up to be a confident, capable and kind young woman. I bet you did too.

From the age of zero to eight, everything was going pretty much according to plan. Sure, the preschool and elementary school years have their challenges, but nothing notable to speak of to derail our daughters or our relationship. I hope you experienced this as well.

During those early years, I was a life coach working with new moms who had just moved out of the city. I worked part time and attended countless classes and conferences, then pored over parenting books into the wee hours of the night. Books written by my gurus such as Dan Siegel, Wendy Mogel, Rosaline Wiseman, Susan Stiffelman, Madeline Levine, Rachel Simmons, Lisa Damour and Po Bronson. My girls were happy and productive, and so was my coaching practice, as I tested out (in real time) everything I was learning on my children and my clients.

And then the world of iPhones, Instagram, Netflix and Snapchat came a-knockin'.

Instead of feeling like I had this parenting daughters thing figured out, I had a pervasive feeling of fear, doubt and powerlessness. Quite often, I felt paralyzed and incapable of taking any kind of action at all.

These screens that innocently came into our lives slowly overtook our home. They became the new family members, or at least houseguests that we never invited to stay.

I bet you have had a similar experience or feel as though you are on the cusp of it coming at you like a ton of bricks. Perhaps you watch from the sidelines as your friends with older children try to navigate this crazy world of smart phones and screens.

If you're anything like me, at times you lie awake at night worrying what exactly your daughter is posting – let alone seeing – on social media? Or wondering why she feels the need to take so many darn selfies with her tongue hanging out Miley-style.

And don't even get me started about how much I want to see those Snapchat images that disappear within seconds by design.

Just a few of the fears that may rush through your mind on a daily basis are:

...Will she post inappropriate pictures of herself?

...Are people pressuring her to post/say things she doesn't want to?

...Do people ridicule her online? How does that make her feel?

...Are other parents seeing things she does that I don't know about?

...Do people think I am raising "bad," "mean" or a "fast" girl?

And then come the statistics and facts that are emerging about adolescent brain development that really send me into a tizzy.

A landmark report released by Common Sense Media in 2015 found that teenagers, ages 13-18, used an average of nine hours a day of online media for their enjoyment – and that tweens, ages 8-12, use online media an average of six hours a day, not including time spent using such media for school or homework.

To give that some perspective, that's more time spent online than the average American teen spends either sleeping or in school. Heck, I could drive from New York to Toronto, Canada in just about the same time. Daily.

And the scariest part for me – having studied cognitive development and neuroscience in school – is that current research shows that there is actual shrinkage of the brain that goes on in the processing areas when children are exposed to screens for too long. That includes the frontal lobe that is just being fused during the key tween/teen years as they mature.

These devices, the uninvited new family members in our homes, are over stimulating our girls' nervous systems with their red and blue light and training their brains to crave "quick fix" information and visuals. While our girls think it's "their life" or "the only thing that makes them happy," in reality, engaging with media so long and so deeply is doing exactly the opposite.

Perhaps you already intuitively know all of this.

You also intuitively know that parenting from fear isn't a very productive place to be, but you aren't sure where to find the answers.

Every day the headlines bring us terrible news as it relates to our kids and their screens. They highlight yet another teenager who killed himself or herself because of cyber bullying, or it's yet another story about a young girl who brought shame on her family and ruined her life because she sent a naked picture to a friend that asked, and now both teens face criminal charges. Each time a story breaks, it seems, you hear the parents of those kids say something like, "We hadn't realized how bad it had gotten." You wonder, will you?

As you lie awake in the darkness with all these thoughts rushing through your mind, what do you think about?

Do you wonder if that could be you and your child? I bet you do.

Well, it won't be you. That is not your destiny.

You are acting, right now, toward a different one. Do you have that?

I'll say it again. That is not your destiny.

You don't have to be part of that conversation. You can choose differently.

You can be part of our conversation, and you have already taken the first step toward joining it – you're reading this book.

No more worrying about how you are going to manage your daughter's social media life, nor passively watching from the outside your daughter's (over)usage of the medium. You are ready to reconnect with your girl, create healthy and productive rules for screen usage, and go back to the basics to help her develop a positive self-image.

No more helicopter parenting where you hover in areas where you darn well know you don't belong. Crashes and all.

We're taking you back to the basics. Hitting a reset button, so to speak. Reconnecting you with yourself, your daughter and your home life.

Your new version of parenting is one in which you will stop focusing on the fear and unknowns, and instead start focusing on:

- Building trust based on a strong foundation of family values

- Creating a comfortable connection between the two of you

- Making family time memorable, engaging and fun

- Providing opportunities to teach and practice critical life skills

Like Glinda in The Wizard of Oz, you will help your daughter see that together, "You had the power all along." And, as a parent, you do too.

It's time we take you back to those wonderful dreams you had when you first heard "It's a girl!" This time, however, you have some hands-on experience behind you. Some trial and error, some soaring success.

You know better.

You know to watch out for the obstacles, road blocks and distractions that life will throw at you. You will remain steadfast with absolute focus on what you want for your girl and your family.

Because it feels unfamiliar when dealing with the platform of social media (the popular new family member, with all its elaborate games and sticky-site tricks) you freeze up, hide and forget to bring your "A" game.

Not anymore. This is your house.

Stay strong. You can do this. You are a smart and capable parent.

You have more influence than you think, even now you can play an active and irreplaceable role in building confidence, a positive self-image and connection with your daughter.

We want so much for our daughters, yet feel so afraid of the influence that social media and these screens have on them. Combine that with how busy we are in our daily lives today, and you can easily understand why you are feeling so stuck and powerless.

Today all of that ends for you.

I have been where you are, and I can assure you that there is a way out. Better, it won't take you countless hours, weeks, months and years to invoke. You won't have to give up your life to monitor your daughter's technology usage or destroy your relationship with her in the process. In fact, by following the tenets of this book, you will find that you develop a stronger relationship with your daughter and are well on your way to building a better you already.

That is, as long as you follow each and every little thing I say to do.

Otherwise you're doomed!

I am kidding. You knew that, right?

You will stand by your daughter(s). Sometimes your presence will be hidden, sometimes more visible. A kind and all-knowing guide. Just like Glinda was there for Dorothy in the Wizard of Oz.

Social media is not going to ruin your daughter. This book will help that statement, that desire, become a reality for you.

As your guide toward a life of ease, family connection and fun, you can count on me to help you recapture the idealistic dreams, new mom excitement, joy of facing new milestones and experiences, and even lighten the mood when things get intense.

And they will.

It is never too early or too late to start doing things differently.

You can bring the ideas that lie ahead in this book, and in my class (more of that at the end of the book), into your home and your family life, no matter what ages your daughter, her friends, and/or your other children are right now. Elementary school-aged, adolescent or college-aged, the same principles apply. In fact, my clients and I (for my own family) revisit these themes time and time again as we all grow and change.

Learning to live with life's messiness is important for you and your daughter(s).

In life, we get what we tolerate. As of now, you are done tolerating social media and screens having more influence over your daughter than you do.

So how about we start with this simple statement: You are not in control.

Let go of the need to be in control and to fix (or prevent) everything.

Stop listening to everyone and no one at the same time.

You have the power inside you to affect change in your family's world without feeling or creating that suffocating need to be in control of everything.

I imagine you learned this the day you even began to think about starting a family.

You have faced challenges from the very beginning, and you have grown from them, after all. Perhaps you got pregnant before you intended, or it was a long hard struggle. Or maybe potty-training or pre-school separation didn't go as you expected. Whatever that moment was for you when you first acknowledged, "I am not in control," let's go back to it.

In the busyness of our lives, we often forget this simple idea. In our culture, perhaps we are even encouraged to believe we have a lot more control over what happens in our lives by our seemingly limitless choices.

Yes, I will say it again.

You. Are. Not. In. Control.

You never were and you never will be – and therein lies your first lesson.

See, wasn't that easy? You're learning something already and we're not even finished with the introduction.

You may not be in control of this situation, but what you do have is the power. Your personal power, your leadership and your influence, which is greater than it may seem.

"You had the power all along" and you still do.

Yes, you can build a better "you," but the first step is simply letting go of the fear and your reactive need to be in control of everything your daughter sees and does online.

You can't protect her entirely from getting hurt, seeing things that scare her or the day when others are talking and criticizing her behind her back.

What you can protect is how much influence you let the outside world have upon her, and who ultimately gets to teach her the values she will carry in her heart.

So go ahead, grab hold of the golden scepter and let's begin this journey together.

Like Glinda, you are kind, compassionate, brave and clever, too. You can show your daughter in time that even when she can't see you, that you are right there by her side: protecting and guiding her.

Not controlling her – protecting her.

Not shielding her from failure – protecting her.

So she may grow into the beautiful flower she is destined to become.

Yes, you can embrace social media and provide the antidote to all the scary, confusing and mean spirited things she sees and perhaps may do on these ever-changing platforms.

With this book as your guide, you will release your own fear and replace it with a sense of confidence and ease.

You got this. I promise.

Your uninvited guest is just that – a guest – in your home.

With a little bit of focus:

- You will set up boundaries to help your daughter(s) feel safe.
- You will provide the foundation for what she holds in her heart.
- You will role model the character, behavior and values you hold dear.
- You will help her learn how to communicate in real time.
- You will help her become her own leader.
- You will be by her side as she makes mistakes, and in turn builds resiliency.
- You will teach her the power of her own thoughts and beliefs.
- You will help her attract that which she wants into her own life, and make choices to remove that which detracts from her life, too.
- You will show her the beauty in believing: in family, herself and the universe!

After all, "There is no place like home!"

Let's get started, "Dorothy."

Chapter 1

GROWING BEYOND A PLEASER
TO BECOME A LEADER

Building Confidence From the Inside Out

I have always been smart enough, pretty enough, athletic enough and well-liked enough to feel confident in most situations.

I have a home in suburbia that I share with my three kids, my adoring husband, and our dog. I have a successful private practice in which I work with families on building confidence through communication and leadership skill training. I often speak in front of large groups of people about parenting, building confidence and leadership skills in girls. I do all of this with ease.

If you met me for the first time at a cocktail party, you would probably think to yourself. "Wow, that girl has got it together." "She sure is confident," you might say, and therein lies what I always felt was my dirty little secret.

Ever since early childhood, I had this pervasive feeling that I was not "enough." Sure, I had all the outside appearances and performance trappings of a confident girl, but deep inside I never really believed the feedback the universe was giving me. I spent so much time outwardly focused – trying to please and impress others with my academic achievements, athletic abilities, physical appearance, and ladylike social skills – and I never spent much time looking inward.

I did not build my confidence on any solid foundation. Nobody is to blame for this. In fact, I didn't even fully realize it until my daughter was born, and it brought a flood of emotions to feel that piece missing.

I asked everyone and looked everywhere for answers. No one could show me the way. It had to come from within me. I have a sneaking suspicion that this may ring true for you too. You, like me, show the world what you want them to see. A confident, capable, courageous and caring (wo)man. We even believe it ourselves, until something pokes a hole in our solid exterior. Daughters poke these holes. In fact, they can leave us with big, open, gaping wounds. Our insides exposed for all to see.

Even right now, as you are reading this book – which I already know deep in my soul will help countless parents and young girls – the critic inside my head keeps popping up and asking, "Why you, Laurie? Why are you to be their guide to tame the social media beast?"

I pause. And I think.

The insecure child inside of me wants me to run. "Run, Laurie, run. This book publishing stuff isn't for you!"

That insecure child that still lives inside of me wants to protect herself from disappointing others, failing, and/or making herself vulnerable to outsiders. She built her confidence backwards: from the outside in. She lost sight of her own strength and natural intuition as she was so busy trying to avoid making mistakes, pleasing others and appearing to have it all together.

She comes out even now when I am faced with tough decisions that most often involve some level of risk and possible failure.

I, like so many women and girls, have always equated my "likability" to being confident. People like to be with people who are easy and fun to be around, or at least that was the message many of us girls receive. Be likable – it's that simple. And if you can make being "likable" look effortless, well then you've got yourself one perfectly-formed "good girl." But being universally liked and pleasing everyone, as you hopefully know by now, is an impossibility.

When your goal is to be "liked" by all, you are forced to disconnect with your internal compass and voice. And the more "great" you are told that you are, the more you feel that you have to be great. All the time. That's a lot of weight to carry.

Like cars that go on automatic drive, so do we humans. Playing out the programming of our childhoods without question, acting on the knowledge and experience we came to know as our truth. We grownups tend to continue to do and believe what we were told to do and believe when we were children, and we never really evaluate whether it still applies or makes sense for us in our adult life. (This is especially true when it comes to the beliefs we no longer even consciously realize we carry, but more on that later.)

That doesn't serve us well when it comes to parenting our girls.

We adults need to get off the road from time to time and evaluate the thoughts, beliefs and rules of behavior we have been carrying with us since childhood. After all, how can we teach our girls how to have a positive self-image when we aren't even quite sure we know the road to get there?

It became very apparent to me, when I had my first daughter, that I needed to get off the road, shift out of automatic drive and do my own internal social and emotional skill building. In turn, I could build my confidence the right way, from the inside out. That way I could role model for my own daughter what real confidence looked like.

And that is when my Girls Leadership journey began.

As I set out to get to know myself –so that I could role model for my daughter what confidence, leadership and compassion looked like – I found my truth.

My truth was that I wanted to help girls of all ages build confidence from the inside out, not the other way around.

Once my discovery about what lights me up inside was illuminated for me, I realized my high profile job in the entertainment industry – the one that impressed other people, but no longer me – didn't suit me anymore.

So now, instead of allowing that insecure inner child's words, the one that are telling me to run, take hold of me, I know to simply notice her chatter. I notice that she comes from a place deep inside of me. A place of fear, and an insecure and urgent adoption of the mindset that "good girls please others." But now, I can stop and notice the fear in the adult situation, and choose to change my thought. I change it to something that serves me far better.

I say to myself with confidence, "Who better than me to write this book?"

As an educator, author, certified life coach, I see firsthand what your lives look and feel like. It was my own life, too, before I chose to take the reins.

I am in the trenches with you, maybe a step or two ahead, and that is exactly where you want your guide to be. As Martha Beck always says, "You have to live it to give it." And live it I do – every day – with my clients, my two girls and my son (who, by the way, also benefits from these important lessons).

My daughters aren't perfect, my family is not perfect and my clients still struggle with themselves, their daughters and their families at times, too. What we all share is a sense of connectedness and calm knowing that whatever life throws our way we can handle.

We, along with countless others, are doing our best to incorporate the ideas and principles set forth in this book. We try things, we allow space for change and imperfection, we get feedback and we learn. Most of all, we believe in ourselves, and in what we are doing as effective parents.

Won't you come join us?

Chapter 2

WE ARE ALL IN THIS ...
TOGETHER

As of late, the topic that I've noticed coming up often with my clients was technology and social media's place in their daughter's life. "It's ruining our family life," they exclaim, and their fear is palpable.

My clients, like you, are highly educated, successful and emotionally intelligent adults – yet they all had this pervasive sense of powerlessness over the little screens that proliferated among their teens and tweens.

As I watched them search for more parental control technologies and clamp down on rules of media usage in their homes, I noticed that this was coming at the price of their relationships with their daughters, their families' wellbeing, and their sense of calm and peace.

So I did what I do best: I set out to find the antidote to this problem. And that is exactly what this book, and my workshops and private coaching, is all about.

The goal of this book is to provide you some easy to understand, highly actionable things you can do to begin to release your fears surrounding social media, reconnect your family, and help build confidence in your daughter. Confidence isn't necessarily the obvious antidote to your daughter's craving for social media connection, but it is proving to be a vital ingredient in growing up surrounded by 24/7 digital connectedness and making constructive and healthy choices.

If you are anything like me, you often wish that social media would just go away. Sure I enjoy a good Instagram post from my favorite celebrity or brand, but when it comes to my children, I wish it would just go away. But it won't. And that's why we are here, facing it together.

They say, "Keep your friends close and your enemies closer," and that is exactly what the second lesson in this book is about (remember the first lesson was reminding you that you were not in control).

I am suggesting to you at this point that you collect as much data as you can about how your daughter is using social media and what she is doing on it.

Note: If you already consider yourself pretty social media savvy, you can skim through these pages. It is an ever-evolving space, with a wide array of apps and platforms, and different kids are drawn to different spaces.

When we were buying our home in suburbia, we were told by the real estate broker that we were bidding against another family. We didn't know anything about them at the time, but we knew that we had a much better chance of "winning" the house the more we knew about the family.

Things like …

Were they tidy? Were they loud? Did they have kids? Pets?

Do they like to throw big parties every weekend?

What negatives do they possess that would make us more appealing?

You get where I am going with this, right?

Of course you do, we already established how smart you are.

Well, you need to do the same reconnaissance on your social media "competitor" if you want to win back your "house" and the attention of your girl. It will take a little time, but it's worth it.

Social Media Basics

The first thing you will want to do is learn the basics of social media if you don't already know them. You will want to learn what are the most popular apps that your daughter and her peers are using. I suggest you look online for this basic information, and then after that, go ahead and ask your daughter. In talking with her about social media on her own terms, you will be showing her that you are interested in learning more about things that she enjoys. You can tell her that you are figuring out how to build it into your family and school life so you can stop fighting about it all the time.

Here's a quick snap shot of current popular items to get you started:

Apps come and go, however, the tenets that follow will apply to any social media your kids are using. This approach to building strong relationships is timeless, even if the apps aren't. The vehicle may change, but the reason kids use them doesn't — they want to be connected, they want to feel important and noticed, and they want to individuate from you, the parent. This is all totally normal!

- **Instagram.** A mobile social networking service where girls share photos and videos either publicly or privately to others. More followers = More popular and quite often they don't even care who the people are. (90% saturation amongst higher income households).

- **Snapchat.** A mobile messaging application used to share photos, videos, text, and drawings wherein the messages disappear from the recipient's phone after a few seconds. Teens love it for the ease with which they can connect with others in real time and **Snapstreaks** are all the rage — they send "friends" a Snap each day in order to be able to keep their streak alive (Also, 90% saturation amongst children at the highest income bracket).

- **Twitter.** A social networking service that enables its users to send and read short 140-character messages called "tweets." A popular commercial platform, teens read tweets and follow handles and conversations, usually surrounding topics like celebrities and pop culture.

- **Texting.** Teen girls, 15-17, send an average of 50 texts per day, while those 13-15 years old send an average of 40 texts per day. Teens form group texts to talk about parties they are attending, what they are wearing to school, and other things. Being left out of a group text is a huge stressor for some young girls.

- **Video making communities** like **Musical.ly and Triller** allow girls to create, share and discover celebrity quality music videos.

- **Facebook.** Not considered that cool amongst teens, because parents "hang out" there. Kids make alias names for themselves on Facebook as they have heard that teachers, college admissions folk, and potential employers check it regularly.

- **Pinboards.** Examples are **Pinterest and Polyvore**, these are used to "pin" images, videos, text, and more onto virtual bulletin boards that can be viewed and shared by all.

- **Sharing Apps.** Forums like **Ask. FM, Yik Yak and Kik.** These sites allow users to ask questions or post confessional text or images anonymously. Note: These apps are no good, no good at all.
- **Video Chat.** Apps like **House Party, Oovoo, Facetime and Skype** allow teens to see their "friends" on camera and to talk. An Oovoo study session in your daughter's bedroom might just have up to 12 people on it. Pop your head in sometime and take a look at her screen. Its format looks just like the visual in the opening song of the Brady Bunch.
- **Video Streaming.** Apps like **Netflix and YouTube.** You may have noticed that your daughter rarely watches television anymore, preferring short clips on You Tube or shows on a streaming service such as Netflix. Note: It has become social currency for girls to know, talk and post about their Netflix viewing.
- **Secret Apps.** Apps like **Best Secret Folder and Ky-Calc.** When kids want to hide private photos, they may do so with an app that displays an icon like a calculator or "My Utilities" so no one will know there are private photos hidden in their phone.

After you've done your initial fact finding, you will want to understand how these social media apps work and what exactly your daughter likes about them so darn much. This way you will know what you are up against as well as gain some respect for what exactly is so intoxicating for your girl.

For example, she might say:
- **Snapchat** is fun, silly and makes her feel connected to friends and people she wishes she was "better" friends with.

- **Instagram** makes her feel special when she is posting pictures or videos of things that she believes her "friends" will think are cool and that represent who she is and what she's doing.
- **Netflix** is an escape. Binge watching shows like Gilmore Girls, How I Met Your Mother, and Grey's Anatomy provide a safe platform for them to talk with "friends" as well as helps them unwind from their overly scheduled days.

Interesting, right? Realistically, despite all the fear that the media (and I) are throwing at you, social media and all the screens we are using so pervasively have both positive and negative aspects to them. The key is to know what she is doing, and notice what comes up when you do.

Next, you'll want to ask your daughter what she thinks the drawbacks and dangers are with the social media apps she is using. Note: You may first want to do some research yourself as well.

Some things she may recognize are:
- **Snapchat** pictures and videos are not private. People can take pictures of a "snap" and there are apps now that can do so. There are many pitfalls in this false sense of privacy. The pressure to send Snapstreaks to people daily takes up countless hours of time and has an addicting and competitive nature. User beware.
- **Instagram's** pictures of beautiful people, bodies and experiences often leaves users feeling bad about their own life in comparison. And the notion that half of the pictures aren't even "real" as people have edited them or created scenarios to make things look better than they are. That can be very hard for someone to see 24/7.

- **Netflix** can be a time suck. Before your girl knows it (or you for that matter) she has watched all 208 episodes of How I Met Your Mother and has forgotten to study for her Social Studies quiz. Yikes!

With that platform primer under your belt, let's stop talking specifics and start thinking big picture. That way we can start working on the antidote to some of those things that you believe are getting in the way of your daughter becoming the confident leader that she is destined to be.

Note: In my Free Stuff section on my website you can find the most current information on popular apps in my **Social Media 101 Cheat Sheet.**

Again, the more we know about the other "buyer" (of our daughter's attention), the more we can make what we have to offer more relevant and compelling. And the more we can unwind some of the possible damage the buyer may do to "your" property the better.

10 Ways Online Media Usage Is Hurting Our Girls:

1. Their language skills are being lost, since they are always tex-ting and writing short format messages. They are using social media to avoid having direct and hard conversations.
2. Outdoor activities, games and their teachers are seen as bor-ing compared to the stimulant of online games and apps.
3. They are losing the essential human way of relating to others through eye contact, touch and physically just "being there" for support.
4. They have lost the ability to connect on a deeper level when something sensitive happens to a friend and take on

avoidance behaviors citing that they feel "weird" and "awkward" discussing sensitive topics on the phone or in person.

5. They have lost the capacity for solitude and their natural curiosity. They are always looking at their screens when they find a moment of down time or quickly turning to their screens for the "answer" before they even have a chance to ponder anything in silence.

6. Their frustration tolerance and patience is very low due to usage of screens and the ability to get "quick fixes" of information and "immediate" connection.

7. Social media has stimulant-like effects that bring about a hyper focus in our girls which is often followed by a crash, as well as causes them to lash out at others when interrupted. The ups and downs create a drug-like effect on them, exaggerate their emotions and take a toll on their general wellbeing.

8. The constant comparing themselves to others is hurting their self-esteem and overall happiness. Girls are using it as way to boost themselves up when they don't really feel good about themselves inside. They are burying their real feelings and because everyone around them is editing the bad stuff out of their social media "stories," girls have no barometer to use to see that others are feeling the same way as them. Research shows 74% of girls say they use social media to make themselves look better, more fun, funny and popular.

9. Girls' identities are becoming so fused with their virtual cyber life that normal development is often being stunted or interrupted and social media usage is often leading to restricted interests outside the home.

10. Now with social media, the "Keeping up with the Joneses" concept has another component. Our girls have to contend with everyone posting their highlights reel, and a much

larger pool of people to compare against (rather than just the girls in their classes or neighborhoods, like when we were that age). Your girl feels pressure to go out and "do more cool things." Social media has elevated the art of doing, seeing and eating new things to a must, leaving our girls feeling jealous and hungry to attend Coachella, visit that cool new ice cream store in NYC, etc.

Make Social Media Work For You

As you can see, online media is reshaping and affecting our young girls' lives. Forever changing childhood and adolescence for our girls, and the generations which will follow.

But it's not all doom and gloom, as I stated above. Truth be told, social media and the amazing technological advances that are happening at lightning speed are adding real value to our lives. Social media is helping our adolescents feel more connected to each other during those years when it's necessary for them to begin to individuate. So what if our girls are texting their crushes instead of passing them notes at their desks, or finding out what the weather will be that day by following their bestie's Instagram weather report feed.

Change can be good. You just have to be smart about it.

You need balance.

Together we have the opportunity to significantly impact how your daughter sees herself and interacts with the world around her. Teach her how to communicate now, during these key tween/teenage years, while her frontal lobe is still fusing together–and you'll see how it pays off in spades in the years to come.

Offer your girl the tenets laid out in this book — and your attention — now, while she is young, and you will see her confidence soar.

Maybe she will send her pricey dish back at a fancy restaurant because it is not what she asked for, or will walk into her boss' office and with strong body language and good eye contact ask for that raise that she knows she deserves. Maybe even sooner than you think, she will have the courage to say "No, I am not interested," when she is at that fraternity party in college.

That's our big picture goal here.

We need to reverse this upward trend of anxiety, depression and dropping out of college because it's all just "too much." We need to prepare our girls for the path rather than try and prepare the path for our girls. We need to remind our girls that home is where the heart is, not just where her laptop lives.

My role here is to provide you with support, guidance and creative ideas on how to build confidence in your daughter and help you let go of your own fears surrounding social media and other things that feel out of your control.

I have spent the past 15 years developing the material that led to this curriculum, and I can't wait to share it with you. So won't you stay the path with me, in honor of your daughter?

It is my promise to you, like Glinda to Dorothy in the Wizard of Oz, that when you stand by your daughter as she goes through the scariest scenarios you can think of involving social media, and you unwind and decode the troublesome things that she is encountering — cyber bullying, being left out, saying and seeing inappropriate things — you both will come out stronger for it, and use home as a place to turn for comfort and growth.

Here is how things are laid out for the next hundred or so pages. In the first half of the book, we are going to help you think about the right boundaries and rules of usage as it relates to technology in your home.

Then with that in place, we can start to create the right environment for your daughters to thrive. We are going to help you get crystal clear on what your family stands for, help you find ways to reconnect as a family, and make your home life more fun.

Next, we ask you to take a dive into your own psyche and clean up some of those old battle wounds from childhood. That will enable you to be cleaner in your own thoughts and role model the behavior you want to see in your daughter. So often, we don't even notice that we are role modeling behaviors that are not in line with our values. Our girls are watching and listening, intently.

After this, we are ready to tackle communication, relationship and leadership skills – for both you and her.

Next, we'll discuss the importance of making mistakes and having a growth mindset.

The book ends with us discussing some ways to bring more positive thinking into everyone's life to get the results we desire. When you focus on what you *want,* everything changes.

Phew – sounds pretty darn exciting, huh? Let's get started.

Chapter 3

BOUNDARIES BRING
BRIGHTER DAYS

Imagine this is a picture of your home.

You will notice that all the windows and doors, and even the chimney, are left wide open. Doors and windows just swinging with the breeze. Every sound, passerby and insect is invited to come right on in...and they do.

Bugs are flying around, random people are talking and the floors are covered with dirt – so much so, that you can barely see what lies underneath. The house is a mess, and no one is able to take care of it because of all the chaos. You can barely hear your own thoughts above all the noise.

Well, my friend, that is exactly what is happening when you don't create clear boundaries and rules around technology usage in your home. Your daughter is being influenced and distracted by outsiders.

You need to be very purposeful in how wide open you leave your doors and windows. Before you begin to open them to the outside world, you want to be sure to spend some time laying a foundation that has strong walls that connect and support each other; a foundation that supports healthy development so that when those outside influences do come around to your daughter, she has her own thoughts on what feels right and true to her.

This is essential in helping you let go of your fear and the need to be in control at all times. When Netflix, Instagram, Snapchat and more come a-knockin,' you will know she can handle it.

And if you play your cards right, you will be the voice of experience inside her head, and hopefully the person she herself turns to when things really heat up.

Our girls desperately want us to be in charge. It is that plain and simple.

Be an ethical authority in her life – not her buddy. She most likely has buddies. She needs role models and ethical leaders to emulate. Adolescents thrive in environments where they feel safe and know what to expect. They like to have boundaries to bump up against, as it helps them figure out how the world works and their place in it. This is what grounds and anchors them and allows them to take risks and explore their world.

Sometimes we don't employ certain rules in our homes, as it's just easier not to deal, or we fear losing the easy-going relationship we may have with our daughters. I am here to remind you that that type of behavior is not helping anyone. We are their parents, not their friends.

When you lay out clear rules and expectations, you empower her to become her best self. You remind her that you are her parent, and your unconditional love and life experience make you the perfect choice to be her guide.

You will stand beside her with love, wisdom and great resolve.

Quite often, when you hear a film or television celebrity or sports figure accept an award, they will thank a parent for having given them a sense of discipline, strong values and the moral support to stand up for what they believe in.

"Thank you for letting me blow off my school work so I could browse my Instagram feed, post inappropriate pictures, and cyber-bully my classmates," said no one, ever!

I have always loved the metaphor of thinking of our daughters as flowers, and us parents as their gardeners/caregivers.

Our job is to nurture, feed and bring warmth to these beautiful flowers so that they can grow and bloom brilliantly into the type of flower that they are destined to become.

We are just the guardians of these beautiful flowers, we don't own them.

Our role is to guide, protect and love them. Hold them up when they begin to wilt or straighten them out when they fall outside their planting bed.

Our relationships with our daughters should mimic this notion.

We need to protect the sparkle in our daughters' eyes and the innate beauty that they possess. That means setting boundaries for them to bump up against.

Depending on what kind of flower your daughter is presenting as (impulsive, shy, sensitive, anxious, risk adverse), you will determine what kind of boundaries and rules you need to establish to ensure her full bloom.

No two flowers are the same. One may be spontaneous, social and creative. The other, reserved, thoughtful, slow to warm up. Together, let's help them blossom.

For the workshops I have created our own version of Maslow's Hierarchy of Needs in order to better understand the "Back to Basics" concept I refer to when building confidence from the ground up.

Root to Bloom: Creating Confidence.

Note: At the end of this book you will find a link that allows you to access my **Social Media Survival Pack,** which includes many of the one sheets and templates described throughout the book, like the **Root to Bloom Hierarchy** below.

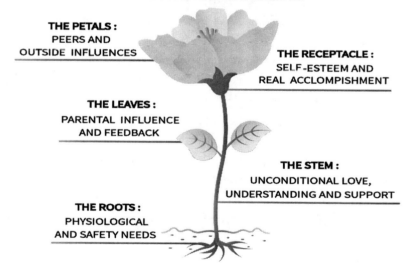

ROOT TO BLOOM :
CREATING CONFIDENCE

THE PETALS :
PEERS AND
OUTSIDE INFLUENCES

THE RECEPTACLE :
SELF-ESTEEM AND
REAL ACCLOMPISHMENT

THE LEAVES :
PARENTAL INFLUENCE
AND FEEDBACK

THE STEM :
UNCONDITIONAL LOVE,
UNDERSTANDING AND SUPPORT

THE ROOTS :
PHYSIOLOGICAL
AND SAFETY NEEDS

Let me take you through the **Root to Bloom: Creating Confidence Hierarchy**.

Starting at the bottom of the flower you see the roots. **The roots** draw nutrients and water from the ground, and enable the flower to stand securely and safely in its plant bed. The same is true for our girls. Our girls have basic physiological and safety needs we must take care of for them, in order for them to even have a chance of becoming a flower. They must feel safe, secure and be healthy in order to thrive.

Ask yourself: Does my home environment allow my daughter to feel safe, secure and be healthy?

Now as we move up the flower, we find the stem. **The stem** represents the unconditional love, understanding and sense of belonging that our girls need in order to blossom into the beautiful flower they are meant to become.

Ask yourself: Do my interactions with my daughter demonstrate understanding, unconditional love and a sense of belonging?

Next is the leaves. **The leaves** help absorb the sun, and produce the food for the flower. Without the leaves, the flower itself would not bloom or live very long. Yes, you, the parent provide the "food" for your girls. The food is your values, beliefs, life lessons and parental feedback.

Ask yourself: Am I providing my daughter with the food that she needs to become her best self? Food that feeds her soul? Sharing my values and beliefs while providing boundaries and the wiggle room to make mistakes?

At the base of the flower is the receptacle. **The receptacle** represents our self-esteem needs. It is the belief of many of my fellow educators that self-esteem needs can only be obtained through real accomplishments. Humans need to experience real accomplishments that involve some kind of a struggle to truly grow stronger. Pair this opportunity for challenge and achievement with a safe environment, unconditional love, compassionate parental feedback and guidance, and the flower is well on her way to blooming.

It is worth noting that accomplishing something that comes easily doesn't give us humans nearly the sense of self-efficacy and agency as does something that we had to work for. If your daughter aces a spelling test or makes a sports team because those things naturally come easily to her, she is not going to build that critical self-esteem muscle we are referring to. We are talking about something that involves struggle, and thus makes the flower (or girl) stronger for having done it. A sense of real accomplishment comes from taking chances, trying new things and accomplishing them despite one's fear and hardship.

Ask yourself: How often do I ever so gently encourage my daughter to try something new, risk failing in front of others, or leave her to "figure it out" so she takes responsibility for the outcome?

Last we find the petals. **The petals** represent peers and other outside influences. Sometimes the petals protect the flower; sometimes, for reasons not in anyone's control, they may cause it harm. The same is true for our daughters. Thus, it is critical to have the roots, stem, leaves and receptacle all doing their part so that whether the petals are or are not supportive, the flower can survive and continue bloom.

When it comes to social media, we parents need to keep an eye on the petals, and make sure that they are doing more good than they are harm. That they are just what they seem to be, as part of the team helping the flower to bloom to its full potential. By no means do we need to stay awake all night in the garden watching over the petals, but we do need to keep a casual and conscious eye on everything.

I firmly believe that in order for your girl to thrive in this crazy, mixed up world of social media and screens, clear rules and boundaries need to be in place. With rules understood, you will have the sense of calm you so desperately want in your home.

Help, Harm and Handle It!

On a blank piece of paper, write down your daughter's name and a description of her personality as you see it, right now at this point in time.

Your thought process might go like this;

Dani is super sensitive and very immature compared to her friends. Any time she sees something scary in a movie or video, she can't sleep. She is very creative, and always wants to do some super exciting art project when friends are over. She can be silly and naive.

Now take that paragraph about your girl, and pull out the characteristics and adjectives you used. In the example of Dani, it would look like this:

Sensitive
Immature
Sensitive to negative images
Artistic
Creative
Silly
Naive

Now write down why you think that her usage of screens and her smart phone is getting in the way of her developing into the beautiful flower that she is meant to be.

That might look like this:

I worry that she is going to see things online that she is not ready to see and that will get into her brain and just sit there. Like I experienced with the movie Jaws when I was young. I still won't go into the ocean very deep! I worry that her friends are saying things online that are not so nice, and she won't know how to handle it, and may say something mean or inappropriate in response or retaliation.

Nice to get that out of your brain and onto the paper huh?

Now go back to your list and make three columns. Label one "help", the other "hurt" and the third one "handle." Under the "hurt" column, write down how you expect her usage of social media/screens will *hurt* her, and then in the "help" column, write down any possibilities for how it may in fact *help* her and then lastly write down how you think you should "handle" things based on the "help" and "hurt" columns.

Since I have a feeling the "hurt" column is more likely to come easier to you, let me give you some ideas for the "help" column. Truth be told, there are some great apps that foster kids' creativity, curiosity and connectedness. Apps that help them make music videos, create artsy photographs, and draw free hand, right on the screen. Musical.ly is one of our family's favorites. There are apps that have games or quizzes about modern culture and history that engage them in an interactive way. Stack the States is one of our favorites. Apps that allow our girls to feel connected to others and share things in a fun and social manner. Polyvore and Instagram are our favorites. And then there's Netflix binge watching. Though it may seem to be mindless viewing, if offers our girls the same social currency that watching certain "cool" television shows or seeing certain movies like we did when we were younger. It allows our girls to feel like they fit in, and engage in light and easy conversations with their peers. Many of the girls are watching shows like Gossip Girl, Pretty Little Liars, Grey's Anatomy, Gilmore Girls, Glee, How I Met Your Mother, and posting pictures, reciting quotes and talking about these shows online and offline. Your daughter feels included if she knows what they are talking about.

Yes, I know that we can find faults with all of the above "benefits" as well, and everyone's priorities may be different. If we are going to get comfortable with the uninvited guest in our home called social media, it's important that we begin to see it holistically and maybe through a slightly different lens. This new lens will allow us to let go of our fears, understand the draw of this way of interacting, and connect more with our girls.

Here is an example of what your sheet might look like.

Note: This sheet is also part of my **Social Media Survival Pack**, which you can access from the link at the end of this book.

SOCIAL MEDIA:
HURT, HELP, HANDLE IT

Personality Trait	Impulsive	Independent	Artsy
How Social Media Hurts	May say something mean by accident.	Goes on sites we don't know about.	Doesn't draw free-hand anymore.
How Social Media Helps		Researches things that interest her.	Taught herself how to build a website.
How We Can Handle It	Explain what good digital citizenship is and how to slow down before posting anything.	Explain to her what is age appropriate content.	Discuss and promote using both platforms as a way to develop her creativity.

It might be interesting, depending on your daughter's inclination, to have her do this same exercise for herself, or do it with you.

Armed with this information, you can now begin to think about what rules and boundaries surrounding social media and screens you need to put in place for your daughter, based on the big picture characteristics and skills you want to protect and develop. Your goal is to foster both the physical and psychological well-being of your daughter.

Family Media Agreement

In my Social Media Survival Pack you will find a very thorough **Family Media Agreement**. The document gives you talking points for discussion with your daughter about what good digital citizenship looks like as well as places to write specific rules of usage for your individual family and child(ren).

You will want to keep your rules simple and, most likely, create a different contract or set of rules for each child, depending on their age and personality. However, the more you can have the same rules apply to all the family members, the better for sanity's sake. Quite often that is just not possible or even what is most appropriate for each child. It is never to early to create a Family Media Agreement. Heck, many of us handed our babies our mobile phones to play with so we could change their diaper(s) with ease. Use the agreement as a launching pad to spark important conversations between you and your girl.

My client Emily had two daughters. The older one, a 7th grader, was never interested much in her iPhone. She'd post a few pictures of herself and her friends walking around town on days off from school, or post a birthday shout-out for a bestie, but other than that, she wasn't particularly engaged. So when Emily's younger daughter got her own iPhone at the end of 5th grade, Emily was caught off guard. She hadn't experienced the hold that social media, Netflix and group texts could have on a child. Her younger daughter's innate proclivity for risk-taking and demonstrated interest in the opposite sex had her worried.

Emily needed two different types of electronics usage policies for her two very different girls. Neither better nor worse, just different. Emily and I worked together to create individual phone usage documents for her two girls, while talking through each girl's individual personality, study habits and level of busyness outside the home. We maintained an overarching theme about their family's values, and kept as many rules as we could the same. When Emily discussed each contract with her daughters, she explained to both of them why some rules were a bit different based on her understanding of their interests and needs, but that all of these rules can be changed in time. Moreover, if they had a real objection to something, they should speak up and it could be discussed.

Her agreement stated simple rules like:
- No phone or laptop usage until backpacks are ready to go and shoes are on.
- Phones and laptops stay plugged in downstairs or in our room overnight.
- Be Positive. Build people up, not tear them down.
- Don't post things from events your other friends may not be invited to.
- Select photos carefully. Only send pictures where you can see your face.
- Don't accept friends or engage online with people you don't know.

Note: On my blog, you can find an article that offers you, the parents, advice on how to create boundaries around your *own* usage of technology and corral all your "screen" errands (i.e. research, emails) to allocated times, so that you can be more available to your daughter and role model for your entire family the behavior you want to see.

Nobody likes to be controlled. Young and old alike. It's basic human instinct to want to assert one's own free will. So why is it that when I suggest to my clients that they have a two-way conversation with their daughters about the screen usage rules, they get so uncomfortable?

It is very important, when sharing these new rules and contracts with your daughter, that you not spring it on her out of the blue or aggressively. Approximately a week prior to when you hope to have your "Family Media Agreement Meeting," mention to her that you've been thinking about creating clearer rules around digital media usage in the home. Let her know that you are on her side, and are not looking to thwart her time spent engaging with social media. Rather, as her parent, you want to be sure that it is not getting in the way of her developing physically, mentally or psychologically. These are real risks when kids and teens are on social media into the wee hours of the night and not sleeping or exercising, or constantly comparing themselves to the unrealistic body images they see.

Once you have created what you think is the "right" agreement and rules of behavior for your daughter, set up a time for you (and her other parent or your partner if he/she is involved) to review the documents with her. As stated above, explain to her that this is a two-way conversation and that with each rule, you will also lay out the reason and end goal for that rule. Remind her that you are on her team, and will have your listening ears on when reviewing the items together. However, make sure that you manage her expectations and are also perfectly clear that you have the wisdom and life experiences to see the bigger picture, and that your job as her parent is to help protect and ground her so that she can blossom. That includes setting up clear rules around time allowed on screens. If you don't think she'll roll her eyes at you and stop listening, you could even tell her about the flower analogy.

Share with your daughter that you are happy to revisit the items on this agreement once a month if necessary. Suggest to her that she make a copy of your agreement, and write on it, making any observations or suggesting changes to the rules that she thinks necessary throughout the month. This empowers her to feel that her opinion matters, and helps her practice key leadership skills. Again, remind her this is not meant to be a punishment. Its sole purpose is to help her structure her time, protect her sleep, and develop good study habits. She also must learn how to interact in the digital world and the real world simultaneously.

As stated earlier, we can't control what our daughter sees on social media. What we can control is how damaging we allow those things that she sees or feels to be to her self-esteem and confidence. Setting boundaries, and setting aside time to talk through what is on her mind, are practices that will change the game for all of you.

I know, I know — right now you are probably thinking that your parents never asked you how you felt, they just made the rules and you were expected to obey them. Well, things are different for this generation, and that is actually a good thing.

We are not talking about a child-centered household. Blech, that's a sure fire recipe for disaster.

You *are* in charge. That is important for everyone.

What we are talking about is creating a relationship with your daughter in which she feels heard and respected, and is able to use her well-developed social and emotional skills to express herself.

A Golden Rule … Slow down and listen to your daughter. I mean really listen–without judgment and jumping into fix-it mode–when she comes to you with the small stuff. This will ensure that she comes to you with the big stuff.

By merely engaging in conversation with our girls about their needs and opinions and in turn allowing them to stand up for themselves via spoken word, we are building the key communication, leadership and confidence skills that we desire for them. This is an important way in which our girls will gain confidence and a strong sense of self.

With her head buried in her iPhone for 3, 4, 5+ hours a day you are not able to do this. She needs to be able to look up and interact with the world and you. That is precisely why you are putting some rules in place.

Whenever possible, state over and over to your daughter that you trust her. State it with true sincerity and explain that you trust her, it's just her developing teenage brain, her frontal lobe to be specific, that you don't trust. Be sure to say this in a funny tone for fear of her thinking you even stranger than before.

Social media plays upon a young girl's angst-y mix of self-criticism, self-doubt and mean-spirited inclinations. Not a great combo indeed. It plays into her burgeoning sense of self and unfortunately deletes the pause button that naturally occurs between impulse and action when in the "real world."

Many of my adult clients say that they can literally feel the charge of energy when they are around their daughters and their smart phones. There she is, madly scrolling through Instagram updates and opening Snapchat "Streaks" at lightning speeds. Her energy feels feverish and truth be told neither of you knows if that charge will bring positive or negative emotions at any given time.

That isn't easy. For either of you.

That is why I firmly believe that we must create sacred spaces and certain times in their day where they must disconnect and recharge.

Some examples might be:
- *Early morning rising.* No phones until "x" hour during the school week and "x" hour on weekends, allowing your daughter to let herself restfully sleep and not get up just to check her social media accounts.
- *During study time.* The mere presence of her phone next to her while trying to study can be a distraction.
- *Mealtimes with family.* If we want the family to truly connect in real time, we *all* need to put away the phones and screens.
- *The short transition time from school to home.* Our girls need time to unwind, chill out and just be. The constant stimulant effect of the screens doesn't allow for this.
- *Sleep/Bedtime.* It is proven that the blue light emitted from phones suppresses melatonin production, and causes a less restful sleep in humans. Not to mention that our girls are going to bed thinking about all the things (positive and negative) they just saw and experienced on their screens, and feeling the intense emotions that have been prompted by the programming.

Sadly, nowadays instead of coming home for a snack, unpacking their back packs and sharing with us parents the goings-on of their day, our girls are burying their heads in their smartphones. They are using screens in every moment of transition, from one thing to the next. Whether it is from school to home, to or from sports practice, a social gathering or driving to Grandma's, they are looking down at their smartphones.

There is no down time anymore for quiet introspection, and they have very little tolerance for boredom. *This is not good.* This is not preparing them for the real world.

You and I know that school, and certainly work, can be boring.

A Golden Rule: Only boring people get bored! Encourage your girls to find things that interest them that don't require another human being or an electronic companion. Organize their desk, make a collage, write a funny story, look through their baby book or some old photo albums.

Let me share with you some of the amazing things you will encounter if you tighten up the hold that those pesky screens have on your daughter and your family.

- You will feel less worried about her future.
- You will have more quality time to spend together.
- She will talk and look up at the world around her more.
- She will complain less that you don't spend time with her as you will be more focused when you are together.
- All the family members are less likely to put one another down.
- She will be more likely to tell you if she is worried or if something bad happened.
- She will be less likely to broadcast her "dirty laundry" on social media.
- Siblings are more likely to look out for one another's well-being.
- She will feel that you understand her more.
- She will feel safer.
- You will no longer feel as concerned with keeping up with the Joneses.

- She will begin to understand that privileges are earned, not an entitlement.

C'mon now—who doesn't want a whole lot of that!

But I do want to remind you that our goal here is media balance, rather than a full restriction.

Common Sense Media, in their groundbreaking 2016 study, found that the parents' influence surrounding media usage is immense. Alexandra Samuel identified three types of digital parents:

Limiters – Parents who take every opportunity to switch off screens.

Enablers – Parents who have given in to their kids' digital expertise and allowed them to set the family's tech agenda.

Mentors – Parents who are guiding their kids both onto the Internet and within it.

Samuel also found that when it came to safety and citizenship, mentorship mattered. Samuel's research suggested that children of limiters were the most likely to engage in problematic behaviors such as accessing porn, posting hostile comments online, or impersonating others online, whereas children of media mentors were much less likely to engage in problematic behaviors.

Below is a one sheet I created as a reminder of Rules for Good Social Media Sharing. It's also part of my **Social Media Survival Pack** that you can access at the end of this book.

One of the goals of this book is to teach you how to think of yourself as a media mentor to your girl. And as stated earlier, you will benefit in turn from following these rules as well. You will notice that your executive functioning feels crisper, you feel more emotionally attuned to others, and your awareness of surroundings in the moment will be enhanced. Not to mention that you will feel more rested from not staying on the computer late into the night checking emails and looking at Facebook.

THINK B4 U POST

RULES FOR GOOD SOCIAL MEDIA SHARING
····· TO ASK AND REMEMBER

✓ Would your grandma want to see that?

✓ Would you say that "In Real Life"?

✓ Nothing is private. Nothing!

✓ Is it true? Is it helpful? Is it kind?

✓ Don't post something in a heightened emotional state.

✓ Is that yours to share?

One of the girls interviewed in Nancy Jo Salles' book, *American Girls: Social Media and the Secret Lives of Teenage Girls* called the world of social media "a second world." One which they love and hate at the same time. In my workshops, we often call social media an "Alternative Universe."

Social media is an alternative universe for our girls. A world outside their "real" lives that quite often feel stressful, boring and pressure filled. This alternative universe allows them to try on different identities, be creative, and say things they may not normally feel comfortable saying in front of someone. They can try on the role of the "mean girl" or the "fast girl." Roles they are too afraid to admit to their parents they are curious about. This is good in the sense that it strips down the pervasive feeling of having to be the flawless "good girl," and ever "likable," but it also poses risks if taken too far.

pending easy breezy time together, without judgment or
:aching involved.
:reating fun, engaging and long lasting traditions.
howing your daughter that she is appreciated and cherished.

se information, images and outside influences are coming
r girls at record-breaking speeds, and we all are so busy
from activity to activity and multitasking, we can no lon-
ly on the simple idea that our kids will just "pick up" the
values we hold dear, and internalize the life lessons that
end for them.
st like Dorothy in Oz, you cannot and should not protect
daughter from following her own "yellow brick road" and
ig the important lessons that she must learn along her own
lowever, what you can do is provide a clear understanding
t values the family holds sacred, thus providing something
to push off from, as she begins to launch herself out into
rld.
d that starts with basics.
clear understanding of what your family stands for.
ice Feiler wrote a wonderful book, *The Secret of Happy
s*. In it he talks about creating a Family Mission State-
When I read that idea for the first time, a light bulb went
ny head.
s, a Family Mission Statement," I thought to myself. A
ent that is filled with words and ideals that represent each
ial family. Brilliant! Hanging that mission statement
ere visible within the home is the perfect way to remind
es, and our children, each day of the key principles which
nily believes.

However, if you stand by your girl as they explore this alternative universe, and help keep them grounded in real life, *you*
and *she* will be fine. In fact, I may even go as far as to say you'll
be stronger having gone through it.

Like learning any new skill, we need to teach our girls the
rules of the road while allowing for some twists and turns along
the way. We want to show them how to color between the lines
without restricting them to the set design. And when they don't
follow the road or color within the lines, it's imperative that you
keep your cool, talk openly, and rely on the solid roots that you
set in place to help you through.

Let's be honest, our parents surely didn't know what we were
doing when we were out and about playing flashlight tag or
hanging out in our friends' backyards. The same things are at
play with our girls, it's just they are hanging out too often in their
24/7 "alternative universe" where the rules of the road are not as
clear and the opportunities for wrong turns are heightened.

With more clear rules and boundaries in place for our girls
and ourselves, we will be able to become media mentors for our
girls. Helping them reflect on ethical decisions of use, proactively building tech skills that will serve them in the future, and
showcasing proper media balance.

If you stand by your girl as they explore this alternative universe, and help keep them grounded in real life, both you and
she will be fine. In fact, I may even go as far as to say you'll be
stronger having gone through it. By putting forth more boundaries through an open dialogue, you are planting your flower's
roots. You are offering your daughter the basic physiological and
safety needs she requires, and the respect, love and acceptance
she needs to blossom.

Chapter 4

CREATING THE

CONNECTIO

In today's digital world, more than ever,
all our might the family relationship and

These screens are doing a disservice
because of the content that they are see
their self-esteem, but also the cost that
smartphone or other screens will have a
with their families.

This chapter will give you tools to u
tionship with your daughter that can h
negative things she sees on her screens,
back to the family.

Now your "uninvited house gue:
Someone that can add excitement and
but will not change the rules and roles

Like Glinda, you are the guide an
forget that.

I believe that four key elements ca
to the home.

- Creating a clear vision for the
  statement.

Beca
at o
goin
ger r
fami
we i
J
your
learni
way.
of wh
for he
the w
A
A
B
Famil
ment.
off in
"Y
docun
indivi
somew
oursel
your fa

"I must share this idea with everyone," I said back then. And share it I have ... for years with my clients ... and now I'm delighted to be sharing it with you.

It's a game changer, and fun to create, too!

The Family Mission Statement and Family Forum

Family Mission Statement

It may feel more spiritual or "kumbaya" than is typical for your family, but trust me, it's good stuff. Having a family mission statement to refer to, time and time again, is a great reminder for yourself and your daughter of what you believe in as a family. That way when life gets busy, or your teenager simply can't listen to one more "life lesson," you can just call upon a line from the mission statement to let your intentions be known.

And here's how you can organize it in your family.

Start by calling a family meeting and getting input from each member. Ideally you want your child to be at least five years old to do this exercise with you, and it can even be done for the first time in families where the kids are nearly grown. Know that it may take several meetings to get all the thoughts down, especially with older kids. However, it is well worth the time spent, because in the end you'll have a list that truly reflects your family.

During your get-together, ask your children what things they believe are important to create a happy, healthy and successful individual, home and community.

What behavior do they see in other people that they appreciate?

What things do other people do, or they do themselves, that makes them feel good?

What words or phrases do they think best describe their family?

Write down everything. You can always go back and narrow down things later.

Things such as asking for what you need respectfully, sharing how you feel, peacefully resolving conflicts, being kind, helping others, working hard.

Try to stick to ten major ideas. Your final list can have more or less, but ten is a workable number to aim for without being overwhelming.

It is helpful for the adults to come to the family meeting having already done some thinking themselves about the mission statement. Bring quotes from books, poetry or famous people in history that you admire to help guide the conversation.

After the first brainstorm meeting, agree to reconvene in a few days. Ask your children to think about some more ideas during that time. This provides a good opportunity to have them notice their own behavior, and that of others, and think about how it makes them feel to be kind, treated nicely, asked to participate and so on.

Continue to refine your family mission statement until everyone agrees that it is complete and accepts it.

Note: When you download my **Social Media Survival Pack** at the end of this book, you will find a few Family Mission Statement templates that you can customize with your own family's name and values that you deem important.

Here are two examples of what you will find:

LIVE LIFE WITH PURPOSE
enjoy life **work hard**
SAY PLEASE AND THANK YOU
SHOW KINDNESS **SHARE**
count your blessings
FORGIVE *love one another*
be happy EAT HEALTHY FOODS
BE DEPENDABLE **SHOW RESPECT**
SMILE *live generously*
DO GOOD AND BE GOOD

Creating your Family Mission Statement together and discussing the very tenets of it, the intentions behind each word, will make an indelible impact on your girl.

Hang it somewhere visible, refer to it when you're looking to have a teaching moment, and rewrite as necessary. The list may grow and evolve over time, just as your family changes.

Now that you have an understanding of the value of a family mission statement, let's talk about other ways to help your daughter feel connected to you and your home.

With a few minor adjustments, your daughter will find great comfort and strength at home. Just like Dorothy in the Wizard of Oz, looking to find refuge at home when things got to be too much, with a few minor adjustments your daughter will feel the same way when the social media storm gets too strong for her.

The goal, a giant *kumbaya* moment where everyone is chanting in unison, "There's no place like home. There is no place like home." Or, whatever reflects comfort and security at home for you. That starts with setting aside time for each other, listening, sharing stories, and understanding what is going on in each other's lives and the world around you.

A great way to do this is by implementing what I call the **Family Forum.**

Family Forum

Our lives move at lightning speed nowadays. I, perhaps like you, would love to go back to the days where time spent together seemed to magically "just happen," but those days are long gone. We traded them in for travel soccer practice, math tutors, dance competition training, dual-career working parents, commutes, and lo-o-ong work hours as our new normal.

Truth be told, we all are moving so quickly that if we don't make an actual appointment in our iCalendars to spend time as a family or have a conversation about a certain item on our "to do" list, it quite often just won't happen.

Yes, that sounds contrived and even pitiful, but in this day and age for most of my clients it's a reality. Like it or not, we must schedule and create opportunities to connect.

In my workshop we call a weekly meeting where the entire family gathers to catch up and review what is on our minds: The Family Forum. In his book, *7 Habits of Highly Effective Families*, Stephen Covey discusses holding weekly family meetings. Our Family Forum is based loosely on his concept.

Once a week, the family sits down and talks about the week ahead as well as any issues, questions or thoughts that are on each family member's mind.

During the week leading up to the Family Forum date and time, each family member gathers their thoughts and questions and writes them down in the Family Forum Journal, so they don't forget what was on their mind to discuss once the meeting starts. The journal should sit in a central location, like the kitchen desk, and your daughter (or son) can have some fun decorating it or choosing one from a store. For example, they may jot down: "Discuss having my allowance raised because now that I walk home after school. I tend stop for a snack along the way," or "Discuss getting my ears pierced on my 10th birthday," or "Discuss getting a Snapchat account."

Each family can craft their own Family Forum as they wish, but generally it should contain most of these elements.

1. **Compliments.** Each family member gives a compliment to each family member in attendance. Usually something they did well that week. After each compliment, the receiver of the compliment must say, "Thank you." This helps our kids practice saying thank you after receiving praise or a compliment, and gets our girls (in particular) out of the habit of discounting the praise they receive.

2. **Articles of Interest.** At least one family member (can be an adult) brings an article or talks about a story they read that week that was interesting to them, and reads it to the group.

3. **Story Share.** A parent shares a story from their childhood. I got this idea when I noticed that whenever my husband or I would tell our kids a story from our childhood, they would respond by asking great, detailed questions. I looked into why this was so, and then read an article by Elaine Reese titled "What Kids Learn From Hearing Family Stories" in *The Atlantic*. In the article she discussed the idea that children whose families discuss everyday events and family history more often have higher self-esteem and stronger self-concepts. Further, as Reese explains, "Adolescents with a stronger knowledge of family history tend to have more robust identities, better coping skills, and lower rates of

depression and anxiety." Turns out family storytelling helps a child feel more connected to the important people in their life. I was sold at "higher self-esteem."

4. **Trivia Questions.** This is an easy and fun way to teach your kids things you want them to know, big and small, in a fun setting. Which president freed the slaves? What does a paleontologist do? How many continents are there? What was Ralph Lauren's last name by birth? You can even give away small prizes, pennies or points as part of this "contest."

5. **Questions, Issues and Answer Time.** Set aside time to address whatever questions are in the Family Forum journal or discuss new things that are on people's minds. Know that you don't have to answer every question or request right at that moment. A simple acknowledgement, like, "Let's think about that and discuss it at next week's meeting," will do. For example, when my client's daughter asked to get a new app that her parents had never heard of, she didn't want to appear as to not know what she was talking about entirely, so she said, "Let me discuss it with other parents and do some research on the web, and get back to you on it." Thank her for asking, and remind her that you will do your best to make it work for her.

6. **An ending ritual.** Each week, The Family Forum should end in the same way. You can put your hands into the center, and at the count of three all shout "Go team (NAME)!" Or, you can do *Pass the Clap* which is a favorite at Girls Leadership workshops and in my family. In *Pass the Clap*, you all stand up and get in a circle and one person starts the "passing" by turning face to face, body to body with the person next to them. It's often nice to let your daughter or another child start this ending ritual, as it is easy to do and makes them feel special. So let's say Robyn, for the sake of explaining this game, is starting the "passing." Robyn and the person next to

her (let's call that person Emerson) will stand face to face and body to body with each other, and at the same time, Robyn and Emerson will clap. No words. They will use strong eye contact and strong body language to say, "Let's clap together in unison now." Then Emerson will turn to the person next to her (let's call him Ethan), and Emerson and Ethan will make eye contact and "clap" in the same way. This should continue around the circle until the "passing clap" comes back to the person who started it. In this case, it is Robyn, and she would be receiving it from the person on the opposite side of where it started. For more information on Pass the Clap, head on over to my blog.

You can do your Family Forum at the same time each week, or mix it up. Just try to be consistent and do it at least once a week. You can have it right before or after a shared meal or first thing on a weekend morning. You can even do it while you take a walk around the block, or sit on the patio. Wherever or however you decide to do it, just be sure to schedule it with everyone, insist on their attendance, and make it fun.

Spending easy, breezy time together – without judgment or teaching involved – and creating fun, engaging and long lasting traditions are great ways to connect with your daughter and disconnect her from her phone (at least some of the time).

A Golden Rule ... We have *two* ears and *one* mouth. Listen more than you speak, and you will see that your daughter will begin to turn to you more often when the world outside gets tumultuous.

Listening + Sharing = Connecting

In full disclosure, the above rule is really, *I mean really* tough for me. I'm always looking to teach a life lesson when all my girls really want is a listening ear. We have an agreement that whenever

I start lecturing more than listening, all my girls need to do is give me the "you're lecturing look," and I know to be quiet.

Sharing with your daughter that you are human and make mistakes is critical to raising resilient girls (more on this in Chapter 8). Enlisting your daughter's help, by having her point out to you when you are caught in a behavior that you personally want to change, goes a long way in connecting the two of you. You are demonstrating to her in real time the idea that all humans make mistakes, and that we all need outside help in correcting them. She will feel like you need her, and she needs you – and she's right.

At first, many of my clients felt great resistance to this idea. They thought it would change the power structure in the family. "If I let my daughter correct my behavior, won't she think she's in charge?"

I assured them that it wouldn't change anything. Try it and watch the magic that happens when you step outside some of the old rules of parenting from your childhood, and step into what sometimes feels unnatural but reflects a mindset of mutual respect.

In fact, lowering the wall just a little bit, so that your girl may see over the top of it, puts you in the exact relationship that you are craving with your daughter. One in which you have an open and honest conversation about the value in making mistakes, asking for help, and demonstrating that we can all choose to act differently no matter what age and how entrenched our habits, once we know differently.

Our girls need to know, and feel intuitively in their bones, that we are approachable, won't overly judge, can be helpful, and perhaps in spite of agreeing with them, will work to understand them.

Plain and simple, our girls don't want us to show up in their lives as the crazy or clueless parent. If she knows that she can share most anything without you flipping out or showing too much judgment she will start to open up to you. Act crazy, or fall into "fix it" mode when she isn't looking for you to "fix it" at all, and she will turn elsewhere.

It really is that simple. I call this the **C and C Trap** — the Crazy and Clueless parent. When my clients hear this concept they often will ask me, "What if she shares with me something that necessitates a punishment or consequence?"

Here is what I recommend to them and to you.

Start by listening to her with your *two* ears. No talk of consequences or judgment until long after the initial storytelling. Repeat back to her what you heard, so she can better process and understand what exactly happened. Then just sit there with her in silence.

Yes, silence.

She and you are not ready for consequences or talk about what happens next just yet, you will get to that. In that moment, just be there with her. Hold the space for all the feelings she has surrounding the circumstance she has just shared with you.

As stated earlier, our girls want us to be in control. Despite what it may look like during those tricky teenage years, trust me, they do. But first, *control* your reaction.

Yes, consequences are necessary when your daughter steps outside the designated family boundaries, so that she learns that her choices have consequences. But you have plenty of time to get to that.

Listen. Repeat Back. Hold the Space.

In time, you will get a feel for how long "later" should be for your daughter, for now you will simply explain to her how glad you are that she shared what happened with you. You will remind her how smart and capable she is, and that you know she will figure it out (with your support).

Believe in her abilities, and she will believe in her abilities. Solve it for her, and she will think she needs other people to solve things for her.

It really is that simple.

When later does come around, explain to her that you are her parent, and in that role, one of your jobs is to help her learn that certain actions have consequences. Help her to understand the connection between making a decision and the consequence that each decision sets into motion, both good and bad. Teach her that good decision making skills are a key leadership skill, and being able to think through the pros and cons of a course of action, and the impending consequences associated with that decision, are an important part of growing up. Whether it be sneaking onto your iPhone and not studying for your science test and thus not doing as well as you hoped – or enrolling in a ballet class that you always wanted to take instead of the hip hop class which all your friends are doing, and risking being ridiculed for it, each decision she makes has a consequence associated with it. And as her parent, your job is to teach her this concept by allowing it to play out in real life. We will go into this more in Chapters 5 and 8 when we discuss leadership skills and the power of making mistakes. Holding firm on the consequences that naturally come with the decisions she makes is an important part of this developmental need. She most likely won't understand this now, but you will see its rewards later.

What she will say she hears:
"You made a bad decision. You are in trouble."

What she really is hearing:
"I am here for you."
"We are on the same team."
"You can handle this."

What you may hear from her:
"I hate you."
"I am never telling you anything again."

So don't let your fear get the best of you, and jump into crazy "fix it" mode when she resists, as it sends your daughter the wrong message. She *can* and *will* handle what life throws at her and you *can* and *will* handle hearing about the good and the bad stuff that comes her way.

So crazy mode is a no-go.

How about clueless mode?

The girls in my workshops also frequently share with me that when their parents are clueless it also keeps them from sharing the ups and downs of their lives.

At times we all want to bury our heads in the sand when it comes to social media, and those pervasive screens. However, please do all you can to resist that idea. Instead, get familiar with what is going on in youth culture today. The hottest social media apps, Netflix programs and Spotify playlists is a great place to start. You don't need to go and make your own Musical.ly account and start doing lip sync dance offs with her besties, but you should understand the things your daughter and her peers want to spend time on.

If you are clueless about what Snapchat is and how kids use it, it is very likely that your daughter is not going to come to you when she receives or sends an inappropriate Snapchat message.

I'm telling you this simple concept works. As discussed in Chapter 2, take the time to understand those things that your daughter "touches" in her everyday life. Make sure she knows that because it is part of her world, you want to understand it. That demonstrates respect. Heck, maybe she'll even return the favor and ask a few questions about why you love that 80's station on Sirius so much.

Being aware of what goes on in your daughter's "alternative universe" and staying connected to her throughout will put you in the right position to help unwind and decode all the shenanigans that can go on over social media.

You will provide the perfect antidote to its negative effects.

People are people, they just are interacting on a different platform.

Truth is, a lot of the issues our girls are dealing with on social media are the very same things that were going on when we were young, just now it's available 24/7, and is at a much higher cost because it's so easy for outside influences to come into our homes without being invited. The kids can't fully get away from peer interaction, whether positive or negative.

Staying connected to your daughter and keeping those windows and doors just slightly ajar will help her get through it. Fear and strict parental crackdowns will not.

Shared experiences and traditions are another critical piece to creating a connected family.

Roseland Wiseman, the author of *Queen Bees and Wannabes,* warns us parents that there's a fine line between "crafting" magical moments for our kids and creating important traditions centered around family. I couldn't agree more.

Indeed, it is not healthy for anyone if we create contrived special moments on a daily basis. This negates the importance of time spent as a family, and puts a lot of pressure on us parents to always be in the role of entertaining our kids. (We all know a few competitive Pinterest moms). However, we do need to purposely set aside time for family events to ensure that we do what we say we want to do – spend time together. With the reality of our busy lives, I am suggesting that you do a combination of the two. If we create some structure and accountability around "spending focused family time," it is more likely to happen.

And we need to get specific on what some of those shared family activities could be.

Some ideas are:

- Play "Chopped" like the Food Network Channel's popular show.
- Host a monthly movie night.
- Plan a themed indoor/outdoor picnic like "Springtime in Paris."
- Have an ongoing Ping Pong or Backgammon Tournament.
- Skip the car wash, and clean the car together as a family.
- Make "slime" and watch the Kids' Choice Awards together.
- Pick another family whose kids match up with yours, and do an annual lobster bake or "celebrity" game night.
- Get dressed up to watch the Academy Awards and drink sparkling apple cider out of plastic champagne flutes.
- Have dance parties in your jammies. (We are never too old for this!)
- Dress in red and have a Valentine's Day meal with hearts and red food galore.
- Host a talent show (parents included).
- Introduce them to some of the games of your youth: Stratego, Rubik's Cube, Parcheesi, Risk, 1000+ piece puzzles.

"Things to do together" is a great thing you can discuss at your **Family Forum** meeting. The more specific you can be, the better and the more excited your family members will be to start making memories!

For example, on the first Friday of every month, everyone in my family agrees to be home early to have a family dinner and movie night. No phones or iPads allowed while watching the movie – strictly enforced, including parents. That ensures that we will be snuggling with each other, not staring deeply into an iPad. Each month, we rotate who gets to choose the movie. Even if Frozen, Devil Wears Prada or Elf is chosen for the 100ᵗʰ time, everyone will make the best of it. The person who chooses the movie that month also chooses what the meal will be for the evening. We rotate between cooking something together that the "host" has chosen or picking a different type of cuisine–like Thai, Indian or Asian–that ties in with the movie of choice.

Try it. You and she will like it.

When kids feel seen and feel that they are "liked" by parents and others, they naturally want to cooperate. This concept seems very basic, but we can lose sight of it pretty easily. We often correct and criticize our kids, all in the interest of helping them find their way. But how often do we share with them the things we think they do well and we appreciate?

> Focus more on what your
> child is than on what
> your child does.
> **Remember, you're growing a
> person, not fixing a problem.**
>
> - L.R. Knost
>
> LAURIE W.

Tell Her — Lucky 13 and Positive Posts

Lucky 13 List is a great way to share with your daughter the amazing gift that she is to everyone.

The concept of the **Lucky 13 List** came about after my eldest daughter had her bat mitzvah. She was 13. At the ceremony, she conducted some of the service, read a section in Hebrew from the Torah, and delivered a beautiful sermon. She did all of this in front of over 150 people, and did so with skill and grace. It was a huge accomplishment that involved hard work, dedication and taking a risk.

During the Bat Mitzvah weekend, my husband and I had the opportunity to share with family and friends the amazing and special young lady that our daughter is. We reflected on the past, shared stories from the present, and spoke of dreams for her future. We painted a clear picture of who our daughter was at that moment in time, and had the blessed opportunity to pledge in front of loved ones our unwavering respect and pride in the woman she is becoming. There was not a dry eye in the house when we were done with our speeches. We wore our heart on our sleeves that weekend, and our daughter took it all in.

After the weekend, many of our friends who are not of the Jewish faith shared with us how special the ceremony and party was (beyond the rockin' DJ and fun giveaways, that is). Special because it offered us the opportunity to stop, reflect and share with loved ones the amazing human being that is our daughter. It provided us the forum for our daughter to hear out loud all the wonderful characteristics that she possesses, and think about what her future may look like. Things parents don't naturally stop and say in the busy lives that we all lead–but really should.

That weekend was the perfect example of the power that a "real accomplishment" can have on building one's confidence, and how important it is for our girls to hear how much we appreciate and believe in them. For my girl, the real accomplishment was her learning a new language and standing up and "performing" in front of friends and family (as represented by the flowers receptacle in my Root to Bloom: Building Confidence visual in Chapter 3). After her Bat Mitzvah, my daughter was forever changed, her confidence taken to a new level.

It is my understanding that in the Mexican community, the tradition of quinceanera (performed at age 15) shares some similarities, as does the Christian rite and celebration of confirmation.

Note: In my **Raising Smart, Savvy, Self Confident Girls in the #Selfie Generation** program we ask parents to create their own **Lucky 13 List** for their daughters, and create a short presentation that reflects on past, present and future wishes for her.

Another fun thing that we talk about in my classes – as a way for parents to remind their girls that they are always there in spirit and cheering them on, even when they can't see them–is called **Positive Posts**. These are secret notes that you can stash and hide in your daughter's (or spouse's or son's) things.

There are two important components to **Positive Posts:**

Rule #1: They need to be short and sweet and refer to something about their character or that they have done that is exemplary or special. A statement that says "I notice you." Something that can help build her confidence. Sure you can end it with an "I love you," or "You're a rock star!" or "Congrats on making the team," but the note itself is meant to encourage and acknowledge characteristics you see in them that reflect their individual amazingness as a human being. Not necessarily what they are achieving and doing to please. Oh, and don't sign it. The idea is for her to just know that it's from you. Always watching and cheering her on. Like Dorothy knew Glinda was there for her, even when she couldn't see her.

Rule #2: You cannot ask the recipient of your **Positive Post** about it. If they bring it up – fabulous, you can smile, but it's far more fun if these **Positive Posts** have an "unspoken" element to them and become a secret that you two share.

Some examples are below:

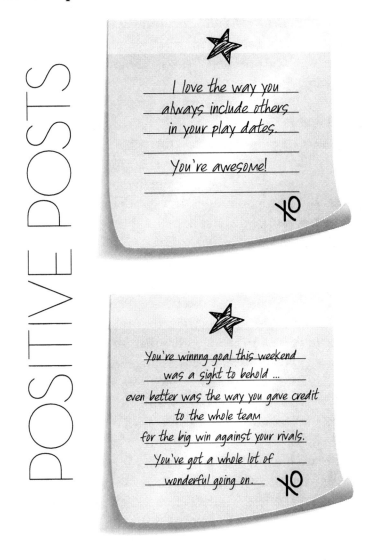

POSITIVE POSTS

I love the way you always include others in your play dates.

You're awesome!

XO

You're winnng goal this weekend was a sight to behold ... even better was the way you gave credit to the whole team for the big win against your rivals. You've got a whole lot of wonderful going on.

XO

If you try and let your creativity flow, these **Positive Posts** can be super fun to write, and trust me when I tell you that they are even more fun for your girl to receive. Try to do it at least once a week, but like anything in life, sometimes things get busy and this may fall off your radar. That's okay, start again when you can. Even monthly is great.

Note: In the **Social Media Survival Pack** you can find blank **Positive Posts** to print out and use to write your own messages. Each page will have two "notes" as seen above. Just cut in between the notes and voila.

Engaged and Present

When we show our daughters that we are engaged and present in their life, with all our heart, they are more inclined to turn to us rather than their friends or anonymous Internet sources for guidance and support. Sure, it's age appropriate for them to call on friends during their adolescence, but for the big stuff we want them to know we are here to help. And if we promise them not to bring the crazy or clueless mom with us when they come a-callin' then we are in for a pleasant surprise.

It is not the parental controls on the iPhone or early curfews that are going to solve your social media problem and bring your girl closer to you, it is the nurturing that we are laying out here in this book, good ol' fashioned listening, being there no matter what, and creating a safe and fun environment called home.

And you will hear me repeat this notion a few hundred other times in this book, because like with our girls, it's hard to know when someone will actually "hear" what you are saying. Sometimes we need to hear the same words many different ways before they actually sink in. Sometimes we need to repeat the same idea many different times before we can change our habits.

So we have to keep saying it. Over and over and over again. And that's okay.

Being a girls' leadership coach, I always have a lesson to teach anyone who will listen. However, my girls are most often not so eager to listen to me as they get older. Thus, I've used social media as a way into their hearts, minds and smartphones. And I share this goofy way of engaging my girls with you, just like I've shared it with countless clients. Be forewarned though, that it helps if you're someone who enjoys pop culture and social media, and consider yourself just a slight bit "kooky" or dare I say "fun-loving," like me. My husband does his own more scholarly version of this.

Meet Them Where They Are — On Social Media

I bet now-a-days some of you feel like you recognize your child best by looking only at the top of her head, right? That seems like the part you see most since she is *always* looking down at her phone. Sometimes it can even seem impossible to have a conversation with her or to pull her attention away from it. Strange as it may be, it may actually be helpful to infiltrate the phone to get her attention.

I'm not saying you should *only* communicate with her this way, but if kids are looking at their phones all the time, let's use that opportunity to be a big influence on what they see. Send witty texts, pictures from things you did this weekend or something you saw that made you think of them. Even a simple I love you statement. When your name pops up in the middle of dozens from friends, she might roll her eyes, but you are staying present in the world she functions in. Just letting her know you're there is a great way to open lines of communication. Don't know what to say? Don't worry, I've got you covered!

On social media, particularly Twitter and Instagram, hashtags (#) are all the rage. Each day of the week has different hashtags associated with it. And girls, boys, adults alike are having fun posting things associated with these hashtags. I decided to take advantage of this fun trend as a means to connect with my girls and send them quotes, pictures and stories that resonate with me and that I want to share with them relating to that day's "theme." My girls never know when one is coming, but they tell me it's always entertaining. I'm not sure if that's a good thing, but I don't mind being ridiculed for wanting to stay connected.

Here's a list of the hashtags that I recommend you use for inspiration. Each week you can send a picture, quote or story related to one, two or three of these hashtags:

Monday	–	#ManCrushMonday or #ManicMonday
Tuesday	–	#TravelTuesday or #TuesdayTreat
Wednesday	–	#WomanCrushWednesday or #WisdomWednesday
Thursday	–	#ThrowbackThursday or #ThankfulThursday
Friday	–	#FlashbackFriday
Saturday	–	#SaturdaySwag
Sunday	–	#SelfieSunday

For example, on Monday you can use the hashtag #ManCrushMonday as your inspiration and send a photo of your favorite movie actor or famous person in history. Mine are George Clooney and the Dalai Lama, if you were wondering. On Tuesday, perhaps you will want to use the hashtag #TravelTuesday and share a picture of a bungalow in Bora Bora that you have always wanted to visit. On #WisdomWednesday, you could share a life lesson with your little lady, and on #FlashbackFriday you can send an old picture of your daughter and you. Saturdays are my eldest daughter's favorite, as I share with her what clothing or accessory item I am currently coveting under the hashtag #SaturdaySwag.

Note: My husband, who isn't into the hashtag thing, sends my kids links to videos, excerpts from articles and bite-sized daddy life lessons through a family group text. That's always an option and quite fun too!

You're smiling right about now, aren't you?

I am smiling too because I know you will find something from this chapter that you can put into place for your family. Maybe the hashtag game feels a bit much, but I trust that you will find something that can help you feel connected and raise the level of easy, breezy fun in your home.

Please know that you don't always need to have a deep conversation with your daughter or a "Hallmark" moment to make an impact. Giving her your undivided attention and showing you care is quite often enough.

I know that you can have more influence over your daughter than her smartphone, and I am here to support you.

Chapter 5

LEADERSHIP SKILL BUILDING HAPPENS AT HOME

Leadership with a little "l" that is my mantra.

We believe everyone has the power to be a leader, and can practice doing so each and every day. And your home is the perfect safe environment to help your daughter flex her leadership muscles. Sure, sleep away camps, adventure trips, after-school classes and sports teams are great venues for building leadership skills, but we so often rely on outside influences to grow our daughters' self-esteem when we can easily create leadership opportunities in our own homes (and for free, or much less cost).

This chapter will show you ways in which you can grab that golden scepter and build leadership skills at home.

While some children may naturally have more confidence in themselves than others, a natural "boldness" does not necessarily make them a natural leader. It has been proven countless times throughout history that anyone can learn to be a leader: extrovert, introvert, popular or painfully shy. Parents and teachers play a big role in helping children grow into their leadership role. Instead of focusing on a child's deficiencies, parents can help develop inherent strengths of a shy or introverted daughter, or a loud, outspoken one. Shy children can sometimes be encouraged to become helpers or teachers to help build their confidence. Rather than labeling a child as too loud or brazen or distant or aloof, we might consider the opposite side of those traits and how they are indeed leadership traits and even strengths.

Be the kind of
LEADER
that you would
FOLLOW

LAURIE W.

It's important for girls to know that being a leader does not necessarily mean being in a position to tell others what to do, it is about leading oneself first.

When you are living the best version of yourself, you inspire others to live the best versions of themselves.

As you may know, many of the most powerful or influential leaders in history were introverts who simply led themselves. But through their powerful individual choices they influenced millions. People like Eleanor Roosevelt, JK Rowling (Harry Potter) and Meryl Streep, among others.

How do you get good at anything?

Practice.

Like practicing playing an instrument or a sport, our girls need to build their leadership muscles through practice in order to get better at it. The latest research has shown that early exposure to leadership opportunities can have significant impact on a young girl's confidence and future.

This chapter is all about your reflecting on what leadership skills you would like your daughter to possess and then finding opportunities in everyday life to teach and practice them.

The Leadership Skills List

Think about what leadership skills and characteristics you think are important for your daughter to possess. Now make a list of them. Use the list below for inspiration and add your items as well:

- The ability to make decisions for herself
- The ability to stand up to peer pressure
- The ability to uphold an appropriate standard of behavior
- The ability to work within a team dynamic
- Honesty above all else
- Friendly, optimistic, funny and warm
- Good decision maker
- Creative, out of the box thinker
- The opportunity to find things she does really well and pursue them
- The ability to assert herself and her own agenda
- Good at problem solving
- Good at communicating and forging relationships
- The ability to take risks and push through fear

- The ability to trust that others and the universe will support them

Now take a look at your list and think about how many of these attributes and skills show up "in real life" on a daily basis in the simplest of ways. Bravery and communication skills show up when your daughter asks the neighbor (the one that never seems to come to her door) if she'd like to buy Girl Scout cookies.

Creativity comes into play when she puts together a dance sequence for all the cousins to perform at their grandparents' 50th anniversary.

Her decision making skills are tested when your little girl is pressed to decide whether or not she wants to try going to a sleepaway camp, and if so, which one.

You get the idea.

So start to notice when she displays these leadership skills, and label them for her. Leaving her with the feelings that they bring forth. Bravery, Creativity, Decisiveness.

And for those characteristics that don't simply present themselves, create or manufacture them to show up within your home life.

Easy, right?

"Nothing good in life comes easily," as the saying goes. It is true in this case too.

To help get things going, I list below some ideas of what you can do to develop your daughter's leadership skills at home.

Creativity

Fast Company magazine says that creativity is the most important leadership quality for success in the future. All companies depend on ideas. Look no further than the world's most innovative companies like Apple, Tom's, or Facebook to understand the value of creativity. It is said that George Harrison of The Beatles once decided, as a game, to write a song based on the first line of a book he saw at his mother's house. Picking one up at random, he opened it and saw the phrase "gently weeps," where upon he promptly wrote his first great song, "While My Guitar Gently Weeps." This little game spurred his creativity, and I bet you could come up with some creative ideas to spur your girl's creativity, too.

One that could be fun entails your junk drawer. C'mon now, everyone has a junk drawer. It could be one of those spare drawers in the kitchen, or the top desk drawer in your child's room. Have your girl go through the drawer and pick out a dozen of the oddest objects she can find. The less anyone knows about where the things originally came from, and what they were for, the better. Then have your daughter create something from the odds and ends. She can create a design with the objects, write a story about them, make a board game using them, anything.

Another idea is to challenge her to come up with a better method to do something that you experience in your everyday life. Like an idea to feed the dog without lifting a finger, or a way that you could clear the grease off the top of a pizza pie without dabbing each piece one by one. Whatever the challenge may be, the idea is just to get her thinking creatively.

Honesty, Trustworthiness and Humility

In leadership, trust is everything – and trust is based on experience. The old adage is true, "honesty is the best policy." Humility, too. So let's help our kids practice these behaviors and help them not fall into bad habits of telling "white lies" in order to avoid a situation or conflict that might be hard for them.

The importance of honesty and humility are hard traits for kids to understand and carry out at a young age, so be patient.

This skill is one that will develop over time. Heck, us adults still grapple with it. However, by pointing out to your girl when she or others are "stretching the truth" or bragging, it can help them start to recognize these behaviors within themselves and others. Tread lightly on this one when pointing out her minor infractions, and try not to make a big deal out of the "white lies" or she may get defensive because she feels attacked. Consider giving her "white lies" a name that the two of you come up with together so she doesn't feel as threatened by your criticism, and is able to notice on her own when the behavior pops up.

Please, no soap box honesty lectures allowed. You can even refer to the family mission statement, and explain how it's an important value in your family that helps everyone develop a feeling of trust in each other. Explain to her how these "white lies" chip away at her trustworthiness. Use an example from her life, perhaps asking her how much would she trust you if you kept telling her you'd pick her up after her dance class at 4:30pm, and then you always came at 4:45pm. As for humility, to spur the conversation, find an example of a celebrity or sports figure that they know and admire. Point out a time when they acted gracious and humble.

When you see anyone you know in circumstances in which they are acting with humility, label it and point it out to your child. Perhaps you want to point out that yes, it's wonderful to feel confident in one's own capabilities or accomplishments; however, bragging about it often undermines the amazing achievement and in the end impresses no one. It is one of life's greatest feelings when someone acknowledges that they are impressed by something you have done without your having to say anything. Having these traits become her natural default is going to take lots of practice and gentle reminders, but time is on your side.

Collaborative Approach

Life is all about relationships, and that requires being able to get along with people from all walks of life. The role of a leader is not to have all the ideas, but to create an environment where everyone can have ideas and feels comfortable sharing them. You can practice this by finding a project at home that needs to be organized and planned, and ask your girl to take it on. The key is that it needs to be something that requires other people's input and participation. Some ideas could be to have her plan a family dinner, in which each family member has a responsibility and she coordinates it. Grocery shopping and all. Or how about have her plan something involving the extended family (aunts, uncles, cousins) whereby she has to send emails and make phone calls to get everyone involved. The key is that your girl has the chance to plan, organize and work with different people working towards the same goal.

A Golden Rule … If you don't need credit for a job well done, anything can be accomplished.

Keep her eye on the goal, not her ego and great things can be done.

Good leaders know this. Now your girl will too.

Good Communication Skills.

The ability to communicate with others clearly and respectfully will help your girl excel in the world around her. We want to role model and teach our girls how to assert themselves and their ideas without coming across as aggressive and thus pushing people away. We will go into much more depth on this in Chapter 7, as it's an essential part of raising a confident girl. Show her how to talk respectfully and with clarity when asking others for what she needs. Mirror for her the importance of listening and then reflecting back what she has heard. You can practice these skills easily in your everyday life as communication (I hope) is always happening. Whether it be asking for a ride to a friend's house or for extra money to purchase something she covets, use each of these opportunities as a chance to demonstrate to her how she can communicate with you and to the outside world with ease. Explain to her why passive and aggressive communication styles are not going to serve her interests, and get her what she wants. You might even want to pull up a video of some of your favorite inspirational leaders, and show her firsthand what leaders look and sound like. This can also be a great opportunity to discuss the influence which good body language, eye contact and a firm tone of voice can have in making one's point.

Curiosity and a Hunger to Learn

Developing your daughter's sense of curiosity and helping her find things that interest and excite her are important leadership skills for her future. Parents can help develop these skills at home by going back to the basics that you learned when your girl was a toddler; the power of why. Remember when your girl used to ask you *why this*, and *why that* every single minute? At first, you relished her developing interest in the world around her. Very quickly, for most of us, that went downhill. If you were anything like me, it became maddening. Well, let's go back to the days when we saw it as a sign of our girls' genius and developing brain, and let's give back the power of "why?"

For example, whenever a question pops into your head, ask it out loud and encourage her to do so as well. "I wonder why baking soda makes your teeth whiter?" "I wonder how far an electric car can go before losing power?" Sometimes we simply don't have time to answer every single question our girls ask, but let's try our best to reward her curiosity and at the very least give an abridged explanation and tell her that you will talk more about it at another time. And then, most importantly, follow through with that promise.

You want your daughter to learn that her curiosity impresses you, and often will lead to your spending time together and quite possibly a few laughs. Share with your girl how curiosity impacts our world, and drives inventors, doctors, teachers and scientists to create things. Explain how things like light bulbs, cars, computers, etc., were born because of someone's questions and curiosity. Challenge her to come up with an answer to one of her or your own questions, and play it out with her. A workshop participant and her daughter were curious as to how long it took for a tulip to bloom. So they planted a tulip bulb in their backyard, and had fun watching, waiting and counting down on their iPhone app each day until they saw a bloom.

A natural bonus that comes from her curiosity is that it will naturally help her (and you) notice topics and activities that interest her. Help deepen those interests by exploring ways in which she can participate or learn more about whatever it is that sparks her curiosity. And be sure to include social issues. Nothing says leadership like helping others. If she keeps asking about the homeless person she saw on the street when you visited the big city over the weekend, use that as an opportunity to help her dive deeper into understanding the social issues our world faces today, and how some of them create homelessness, and let her learn about the ways she can get involved and help out.

Note: I run a great program online called ***How to Build a Lasting Community Service Project***. In it, I take kids step by step through the process of finding a social issue that they connect with, choosing an organization that resonates with them and then finding a way to work with that organization to make an impact surrounding the social issue that matters to them. Whether it be collecting shoes for children in Africa for

Soles4Souls, working at the local food pantry in an ongoing way, or raising money for cancer, doing good is a great way to develop leadership skills.

Good Decision Making Skills

Great leaders are comfortable making decisions and know that there is always a risk at stake when they choose one thing over the other. They also know that the ability to make a swift decision is key, and that you can bounce back from almost any wrong choice. So let's help our girls practice making decisions (and quick ones, too). I sure could have used this practice when I was younger. Though it may seem obvious, take her through your best "Decision Making 101" class you can come up with, and explain to her how you go about making decisions. Maybe you use a pros and cons list, maybe you rely on intuition. Whatever it is, share your methods with your daughter. Ask her what she thinks guides her and others to make good decisions. And like we stated in Chapter 4 on family values, explain to her that it's important to take into consideration the consequences that come with one choice over another.

Organization Skills

Organization is a great skill to have in life. When I say organization, I don't mean a neat bedroom or tidy kitchen sink area. Your daughter is a tween/teen, and it's very normal if she is the type of girl who throws all 20 of her potential outfits on her bedroom floor during the mad scramble to get off to school. However, when she is doing the clean-up that evening (or weekend, dare I say) join her and discuss with her the idea of working together to set up some kind of an organization system in her room for her clothes, accessories and bathroom products so that she can more easily see them and get herself out the door in the morning. You might even want to promise her that she can play her music and be (mostly) in charge while you work together.

Talk through with her how you personally think through and approach keeping things organized, and be honest with her if this is a skill you find challenging. Explain to her why it is helpful to have things organized, and that organized is not the same thing as "neat." She can still have clothing on the floor from getting ready in the morning, but if the room is organized the clean-up and where to put everything after should be pretty easy. Plus, with an organized room, she'll be able to find her favorite blankie when it's bedtime far easier!

Good Networking and People Skills

People like people who engage in two way conversations, listening and sharing their thoughts in an easy manner. Point out to your daughter when you've spent time with someone who does this, and ask her why she thinks that person is so easy to be around. Use this as an opportunity to explain to her how healthy conversations between people have a give and take flow to them. Discuss with her the importance of learning how to start a conversation with someone you don't know, and how to push through that fearful and awkward feeling when approaching someone new. Role model for her what an engaging two-way conversation sounds like and if you think she can handle it, find opportunities for her (and you) to meet someone new.

The Leadership Stance

This isn't exactly a skill, but more of a way of behaving that exudes confidence and shows others that you are interested in them or the conversation at hand. It's a great antidote to all the texting and posting that our girls are doing on their smart phones. The Leadership Stance consists of strong body positioning, direct eye contact and a firm tone of voice.

Her arms should be hanging loosely at her sides, her feet should be firmly on the floor and her shoulders should be square facing the person she is speaking with. Her eyes should be looking directly into theirs and her tone of voice should be clear and firm. All these elements convey that you are confident, strong and take the situation that you are discussing seriously.

Note: For more ideas on leadership skill development, go to my website, join one of my programs or work with me individually. This can help hold you and your daughter accountable for setting up some of these challenges within your home.

In the past, good grades in school were a strong indicator of success for a young girl. However, we are now seeing that keeping your head down and focusing *only* on academic or physical achievement is not enough. And that's a good thing. Having report cards that are covered with A's alone is not doing our girls justice. In fact, along with those A's we want to be focusing on a whole lot of C's, too:

Communication

Collaboration

Commitment

Contribution

Character

Creativity

We want to build her confidence and leadership skills from the inside out. Don't rely on the external world to offer her pats on the back that say "nice job," instead help her to learn to rely on her own sense of achievement, her own list of real accomplishments that required some work.

Feeling inspired? Me too. With a little advance planning and a whole lot of enthusiasm, you can truly build your own Girls Leadership School right in your home.

So grab that golden scepter, and start to practice some of these skills now. In no time, you will begin to feel more at ease about the influence all that social media and screens have on your daughter.

Chapter 6

HEALING AND ROLE MODELING

The most effective way to influence our daughters is to role model the behavior we want to see in them. Period.

You want your girl to be the type of person who asks follow up questions when others are talking instead of launching right into talking about herself? Show her what that looks like.

You want her to say thank you when someone gives her a compliment instead of, "Eew, I look terrible. My hair's so frizzy today." Do the same.

You want her to greet the custodian at school with the same smile and enthusiasm that she gives the principal? Be sure to warmly engage in conversation with the various service people in your life.

You want her to look up from her laptop and smart phone? Well, look up from yours, too.

You want her to post comments and pictures online that are kind and constructive and represent her authentic self. Take a look at your own Facebook page.

And wouldn't you love to see her have the courage to carve her own path instead of following the pack? Consider heeding your advice and start following your own path, or at least re-evaluate your path to make sure it's still the one you are fully committed to.

Yup, it is true. You hold *a lot* more power than you realize.

It all starts with you.

Yes, you.

The best and worst part (and maybe the scariest part) of that is that you don't even have to say a word for that to be true. Our girls are watching, listening and taking in how we treat others and how we allow others to treat us. They pick up on our nuanced behaviors when interacting with babysitters, teachers, other working or non-working parents, house cleaners, in-laws and the opposite sex.

Actions speak louder than words.

But you knew that.

That's why it is so important for you to heal those old battle wounds from your own childhood. Only then can you truly see pieces of yourself mirrored back at you in her eyes.

Have you ever noticed that certain situations that your daughter is in really seem to rile you up, making you anxious or fearful or possibly a little hyper?

Next time this happens, take notice of how exactly you are feeling inside your body. Betrayed, anxious, lonely and/or helpless, perhaps. Now give that feeling a number from 1 to 10 with 1 being "it doesn't feel that intense" to 10 being "so intense I can barely breathe."

For example, many of my workshop participants have shared with me that they feel an 8 or a 9 in intensity when they get that dreaded email from another parent pertaining to something their daughter may have done that hurt another child. They are so nervous and uncomfortable with the thought that other people may think their child is unkind, and might even be judging their parenting, that they will do virtually anything to make those feelings go away, anything. Even yell at, judge and punish their daughter without knowing the full story.

This is very typical of the stories I hear in my workshops.

So why do think so many of the situations that our daughters are going through strike such a chord with you, me and the countless other parents I work with?

It is because these circumstances bring up old feelings that have since been buried, but not yet reconciled from our childhood. Feelings of loneliness, insecurity, embarrassment, nervousness and disappointment to name a few.

Your emotional child is being summoned by the actions of your own child and her friends, and you didn't even realize she/he was still there deep inside you.

Emotional Childhood vs Emotional Adulthood

Brooke Castillo of the Life Coach School explains the concept of Emotional Childhood vs. Emotional Adulthood very astutely. She explains that in emotional adulthood, one no longer blames others or circumstances for the way they are feeling. They realize that they have not been made to feel a certain way by someone else, but rather they are in charge and have chosen to feel that way based on how they respond to certain events and people. Change our thought about a circumstance, and we can change how we feel. That is the mantra and the goal.

Truth is, most of us call ourselves adults, but many of us are still functioning as emotional children. There is no class in which you learn how to become emotionally mature adults. Therefore, if no one has taught you how to control your own thoughts and take responsibility for your own actions (and thus the results), you can remain in emotional childhood forever–or at the very least fall back into it when feeling under pressure. Even once we are taught, it takes practice.

It is not something we do on purpose, most of our parents still function as emotional children as well, thus continuing the cycle.

In emotional childhood, we behave like children: relying on others to take care of us, acting upon impulse, and walking around like victims.

It's time to break that cycle for our girls and ourselves.

Some examples of typical emotional childhood behaviors that you may recognize in yourself are:

- Wanting immediate gratification; impatience.
- Rebelling against the very things you want.
- Giving someone else the job of making you happy when only you can make you happy.
- Saying, "It's not fair."
- Playing the victim and saying, "It's their fault."
- Being fussy and picky over little things.
- Pouting or giving the silent treatment when you feel wronged.

There is no shame if some of these behaviors show up in your everyday life, the key is to start to notice it. Then try to move yourself from emotional childhood (outward focused, i.e. "They did something to make me feel this way") to emotional adulthood (inward focused, "I am in charge of how I feel.")

While it can be difficult to take responsibility for your own emotions, it's also very freeing. If you are responsible for your own emotions, then the words and actions of another person cannot make you feel a certain way.

You get to choose how you feel.

So back to that pesky 1 to 10 scale, and those old battle wounds from your own childhood. By beginning to identify which circumstances elicit strong feelings within you, you can then figure out the thought that is connected to the circumstance that is holding you back. Once you acknowledge your wounds and start to heal them, you can come to support and guide your daughter from a "clean" place. Not one that is still dirty with your own emotional childhood, your own past painful thoughts and responses.

This merits restating: *She is not you. You are not her.*

You are not on this earth to fix things for her, things you didn't get right your first go-around. You are here to nurture, feed and water the beautiful flower that she is. She needs to battle the tumultuous elements herself in order to ensure her own survival.

So let's free you from some of the wayward thoughts that are hanging around and holding you and your girl back.

One great way to do that starts with the simple question of "Why?" and ends with the Thought Police getting involved.

The Five Whys and Thought Police

The concept of **The Five Whys** was taught to me at The Martha Beck Institute. It is a simple technique you can use to move past your frustrations and symptoms, and get to the root of a problem you are having – whether in life or business.

Take Bettina for example. Bettina can't stop obsessing over the fact that her daughter Cleo isn't included in most of the weekend plans that her daughters so called "friends" make. However, Cleo doesn't seem to notice, let alone mind, when she isn't invited. Indeed, she enjoys spending time unwinding at home on weekends. "She's so clueless," Bettina tells me over and over. "She doesn't even notice that they are getting together and never inviting her. It makes me crazy!" She continues: "Those girls can be so mean and she doesn't even see it."

So I ask her.

ME: "If Cleo doesn't notice or even want to join their weekend plans WHY (1) does it enrage you so?"

Bettina: "Because they shouldn't get away with leaving her out."

Me: "Ah, I see", "WHY?" (2)

Bettina: "Because that is mean."

Me: "WHY (3)?"

Bettina: "Because they think they are better than her"

Me: "WHY does that matter? (4)"

Bettina: "Because she isn't as comfortable socially just yet."

Me: "WHY does that matter? (5)"

Bettina: *"Because she doesn't fit in easily and I want her to feel different than I did as a young girl. I want her to be popular and well liked!"*

And there is the golden nugget: the thought that Bettina needs to do some work on.

Bettina's discomfort with her daughter's cluelessness about being left out had nothing to do with Cleo and everything to do with Bettina feeling like an outsider when she was a child.

Armed with that thought we can now bring it to the **Thought Police**. The **Thought Police** is based on a model that I learned when training with Brooke Castillo. It changed my life and I am excited to share it with you. It's classic cognitive behavioral theory stuff.

The model goes like this.

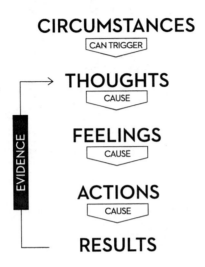

(**Note:** I have recreated this visual from *Self Coaching 101: Use Your Mind – Don't Let It Use You* with Permission from the author, Brooke Castillo – www.brookecastillo.com.)

Brooke defines **Circumstances** as "the things we can't control," which will include other people's behavior, facts and situations. **Thoughts** are beliefs about circumstances, or as Brooke says, "a sentence that is formed in our mind" based on circumstances. **Feelings** are a "vibration in our bodies caused by our minds," and **Actions** are "what we do or not do," and lastly, **Results** are "the effect of action."

As you can see from above, our thoughts drive everything we do. Thus, change your thought, and you in turn change your behavior, and thus your results.

Simple, right? It is—and it's not. I suggest that you read Brooke Castillo's Self Coaching 101 to get the full greatness of this work. However, for now, this will do just fine.

It is your thoughts that are giving you the results you are getting from the universe, not the circumstance or your actions.

Use the **Thought Police** model to find the limiting thought that is affecting your feelings, actions and thus your results. Quite often, we aren't even aware of the thought that is holding us back.

We adults should not underestimate how many of us are on automatic pilot, playing out the programming of our childhood without question. We do what we think we should do, based on what we were told as children, and we have never taken the time now as adults to evaluate whether it still applies or makes sense.

Some examples:

"You should not let people know how you feel as it creates conflict and makes them uncomfortable."

This thought can lead you to avoid conflict and thus possibly ruin relationships as you hold your feelings inside.

"You should put others first."

This thought can lead you to not take care of yourself, thus feeling depleted and perhaps resentful all the time.

"You should provide for your family."

This thought can lead you to stay in a job that doesn't fulfill you, leaving you feeling uninspired and depressed.

Let's try it with Bettina's thought/circumstance. The bolded line was where she started. Which in this case was the *circumstance* of her daughter being left out. The rest of it you will see was just the result and action taken based on her thought about the circumstance.

We can plug in any variable and see where it takes us.

C - Cleo's friends did not invite her to Friday night's get-together.

T - They don't think my daughter is cool enough.

F - Sadness, anger, worry.

A - Bettina points out to Cleo that her friends aren't being good to her.

R - Cleo acts awkward and anxious around her friends, leading them to not want to be around her.

Now, let's plug in a different thought and do the work.

C - Cleo's friends did not invite her to Friday night's get-together.

T - **Right now, Cleo is not jiving with her group of friends.**

F - Calm, indifference.

A - Matter of fact planning around her going to the get-together.

R - Her daughter is at ease at the party, and the other girls enjoy being with her.

Can you see the difference?

It was Bettina's thoughts still lingering around from her childhood that were getting in the way of her supporting her daughter.

An element that is great about Brooke's model is that you can "plug in" whatever piece of information you have at the moment. For example, if you are simply feeling sad, you can plug that into the feeling line of the model, and then work from there. You don't necessarily have to have the circumstance in place to work the model. It is a helpful element, because it gives people more room to find the painful thought, and it clearly illustrates the consequences of believing one's negative thoughts.

I don't know about you, but I always believed that the circumstances in my life were causing me to feel a certain way until I studied this model. The **Thought Police** model beautifully illustrates that this simply is not true.

Again, change your *thought,* and you can change the outcome.

Doesn't that feel like freedom? It should, because who is in charge of your thoughts? Yup, *you are.*

You *are* enough.

You are the boss of your brain.

This is not easy work. Believe me, I know. I live it every davy.

Most everything in life needs to be watched over. Including your mind.

And getting good at anything takes practice. Including the way you think.

Sometimes, in conversations about my life coaching degree, I get the question, "What is a life coach?" I love to explain that "We are personal trainers for your mind."

Armed with **The Five Whys** and the **Thought Police** models, you can now shed a light on some of those outdated thoughts and behaviors that no longer serve you, and help your daughter see that she does not have to rely on external praise to feel like she is enough.

You are (or are becoming) a capable, independent adult, ready to watch your thoughts and live in emotional adulthood. Now that we've got you on the road to cleaner thinking let's talk about some of your actions that you *may* or *may not* be aware of.

Role Modeling

As I said before, and it's worth repeating, we parents need to talk less and act more.

We need to role model the behavior we want to see in our daughters.

> Don't worry that children never listen to you; **worry that they are always watching you.**
>
> - Robert Fulgrum
>
> LAURIE W. ♥

In order to role model behaviors that we want our daughters to "take on," we need to take a good honest look at the behaviors of our own we are showcasing for our girls, both consciously and unconsciously.

Below is a list of things you want to course correct. Some of these may send the wrong message to your girl, and others may present opportunities to start to do more proactively:

Try not to gossip about other people behind their backs and in front of your daughter. If you must get your feelings off your chest, save it for a private conversation with your partner or bestie when no one else is around.

Minimize the negative talk about your other children and/or family members. This makes her think it's okay to speak poorly of family members in front of others, and often points out limitations in them that they may not have noticed. Not to mention, it's just bad form.

Treat everyone who crosses your path respectfully and kindly. You will notice this is one of those "monkey see, monkey do" behaviors. Take the time to treat all the people who touch your life with respect, and you will be demonstrating kindness, compassion and caring to your girl. Everyone wins here.

Try to eliminate swear words. Need I say more? This one I am working on myself, I admit.

Show her you are willing to face your fears. Point out something that scares you, but that you have always wanted to try. Then point out that although it scares you to do "X, Y, Z," you are going to challenge yourself and do them anyway. She will be impressed even if she doesn't tell you so.

Be silly, goofy, put yourself out there. This will allow your daughter to feel that she, too, can "let go" at times and that kids aren't the only ones who get to have fun. It also helps her let go of that drive for approval and living up to the good-girl ideal, and feeling that she needs to be polite and perfect all the time.

Notice the world around you. Point out a beautiful tree on a neighbor's lawn, a painting in a restaurant at or an article that you recently read that taught you something new. Your girl may not act interested at the time, but trust me, she is taking it all in—and learning the value of being curious and appreciative.

Say "No" when you mean "No." This one is important for both of you. Show your daughter the power in saying "No." Role model for her how to evaluate the situation, and then assertively say, "No thank you," if the situation doesn't suit you. If you don't want to volunteer for the school fundraiser, or are not interested in going out on a busy weekend, well then just say "No." Remember, she's watching. Politely and respectfully, of course, but say something. Tell your truth. "No, thank you" will be an important sentence in her repertoire someday.

Be a friend. Role model for your daughter how to be a true friend. Stop by a friend's home with a small gift when you know she isn't feeling well, take walks with friends just to "catch up," and never share your friend's secrets or personal problems with your family.

Share your mistakes and failures. Help your daughter see firsthand that making mistakes (often) is part of being human. Share with her stories of your colossal failures, and find examples of how, quite often, one's worst mistake can lead to their most favorable outcome. For example, maybe when you were young, you didn't get into the graduate school across the country that you wanted to attend. Instead, you stayed close to home, which allowed you to spend three wonderful years living at home and save money, possibly broadening your career choices.

Demonstrate good media balance. Be a "media mentor" for your daughter. Show her (and openly discuss with her) your own struggles with social media and screens. Let her know you are trying, just like her, to find balance — to see friends in person more, and to step away from the computer in the evenings to spend more connected time with your kids.

Along with starting to notice the behavior that we are role modeling for our daughters, also start to notice how you talk about your daughter–both in front of her as well as indirectly about her to others.

Think to yourself before you say something, "Is this going to help or hurt her self-esteem?"

Like it or not, the way we talk about our children becomes their own inner voice. If we keep telling her that she is forgetful and absent-minded, over and over, well then lo and behold she just may start to believe it—and fulfill that destiny for both of you.

Instead of pointing out the things that she is doing "wrong," make a conscious effort to catch her doing something good. Point out when she does something kind or helpful. Mention the mundane things that she does that add tremendous value to everyone's lives and let her know much you appreciate them.

A Golden Rule ... Shine a light on the good things, and leave the others in the shadows. Let her overhear you praising her to others. Maybe you are chatting with a friend while she's in the car, or you are talking with her teacher at school during pick up. Whatever it is, make sure she hears all the good things you have to say about her. Like the **Lucky 13 List** in Chapter 4, this will give her a great confidence boost.

If you are anything like me, at times you are so busy rushing from thing to thing and checking off your own to-do list that you end up rushing your loved ones through a conversation. This needs to stop. To truly have the connection that we desire with our girls, we need to show them that we are here for them. Ready to listen and put things aside for them. Even our smartphones.

I end this chapter with a quote that is hanging in my kitchen as a gentle reminder.

Listen earnestly to anything
your child wants to tell you,
no matter what.

If you don't listen eagerly to
the little stuff when they are little,
they won't tell you the big stuff when
they're big, because to them it
ALL has been big stuff.

- Catherine M. Wallace

Chapter 7

COMMUNICATION IS FOR EVERYONE

Learning how to communicate how you feel to others is one of life's greatest challenges. Learning how to communicate what you are feeling when someone else has *different* feelings and thoughts is an even greater challenge.

I know you and your girl can handle that challenge.

Like we discovered in Chapter 6, there is no school or class to teach us how to move from emotional childhood to emotional adulthood. The same can be said about learning how to communicate how you feel and ask for what you want effectively.

Our girls learn communication skills by watching us communicate, as well as watching other people in their lives do so. Whether it be on television, social media, the playground or at team practice, our girls are picking up communication style cues from all of these outside forces.

In Chapter 2, we discussed many of the negative consequences that social media presents as it pertains to communication skills. With online media playing 24/7, and clamoring for all of our attention, it's even more imperative than ever to teach our girls "real life" communication skills at a young age.

It is foreseeably less likely in the digital age that she will pick up positive interpersonal relation skills without your intentional effort in this direction.

For over a decade, I have been asking fellow educators why most public schools don't teach communication skills in early childhood education. It makes no sense. It is the backbone of human existence!

Maybe, just maybe, a girl is lucky enough to take a class in college on communication, but this invaluable nuanced skill is more often left for our girls to learn on the playground or through a YouTube video.

Well, not anymore. I am going to take you back to the basics, and share with you lessons, skills and phrases that I teach in my workshops and to private clients that you can bring into your home and share with your daughter. Whether she'll be open to learning it from you, at this point in time, may present a challenge. Just starting the conversation, role modeling and slowly bringing these lessons into your home, even if she hasn't bought into it just yet, is a great first step.

The ability to identify how you feel, express that feeling to others, and ask for what you need can be life changing. Girls are often afraid to share their feelings, as they don't want to be seen as downers or high maintenance. The "being likable" expectation of girls is very strong. We have to gently nudge our girls to break through that thinking, as it's at too high a cost later in life.

Intimacy comes when you share how you feel. That is how relationships get stronger. And relationships are the cornerstone of happiness. When feelings are kept inside and not voiced, that is when we see unhealthy and problematic behaviors. The severe end of the spectrum of behavior or health effects of not dealing with our feelings being: depression, self-harm, drinking and drugs.

> If you just
> communicate, you
> can get by. But if you
> **communicate**
> **skillfully,** you can
> make miracles.
>
> - Jim Rohn
>
> LAURIE W.

Four Styles of Communication

Helping our girls develop and grow healthy relationships is paramount. In my workshops I begin our communication skills lesson by talking about the four different communication styles that exist. In any given situation, a person is using one of these types of communication styles. Quite often, people have a tendency to stick with one preferred or default style. By being aware of these styles, your daughter can begin to understand the concept behind "It's not what you say, it's *how* you say it." She can begin to decide on her own what type of friend and communicator she wants to be, and then what kinds she is willing to allow into her life and relationships.

The 4 styles of communication are:

Aggressive

Assertive

Passive Aggressive

Passive

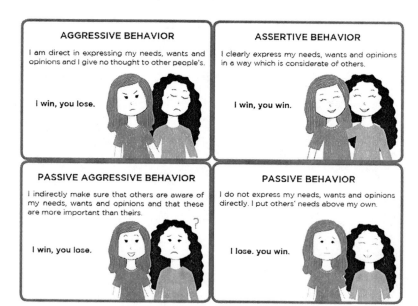

Look at the chart above, and share it with your daughter as well. Here you can see examples of what each mode of communication looks like. When discussing these styles, help her understand that it's important to notice how one's choice of words can make another person feel. In my workshops, we discuss how girls often don't pay attention to their feelings and try to hide them, because acknowledging at least some of them would hurt too much. However, in the class, we demonstrate that having your feelings hurt should really be no different (i.e. shameful) than the hurt you would feel had you sprained an ankle. It needs to be taken care of. If you sprained your ankle, you would do well to put ice on it. You might even ask someone to help you get around until it healed. The same reasoning should be applied to one's feelings. They should not be ignored. Ignoring a sprained ankle will most likely make things worse. The same thing is true when your daughter (or you) hides their true feelings.

Let me explain further, so you can enlighten your daughter as well.

Aggressive behavior can appear in two different ways when it comes to girl culture. Sometimes it's very hurtful and domineering, and sometimes it's less outwardly aggressive, but both manifestations can hurt just as much. Maybe a friend or classmate threatens your daughter, by saying, "I am not going to be your friend if you don't do as I say." Maybe she has experienced someone being more openly aggressive and they have physically pushed or hit her. Truth be told, both leave lasting wounds. However, in the less aggressive example, the weapon is concealed. She is using your daughter's fear of losing the friendship, or not belonging, as the weapon. This behavior can be very hard for girls (and many adults) to see and understand.

It's important for you and her to understand this. Those "hurt" feelings often get buried and cause girls not to speak up. Later in life, whether in work or in relationships, she may not speak up yet again, having carried with her this default way of being in the world. This can come at tremendous personal cost to her career, in a marriage, or even in trying to find the social setting that suits her best.

As for as how to explain **Passive** and **Passive *Aggressive*** behavior to your girl, these are tricky communication styles to maneuver around. Provide her with examples as you see them happen in real life. Show her what passive behavior looks like, and point out how a passive individual often leaves others feeling confused as to what they truly want. Help her understand it is not her job to make other people (friends and parents included) happy. It is her job to make herself happy. Thus if a friend is having a tough time but doesn't share with you what you can do to help the situation, it's okay to take a break, and not assume responsibility for restoring him or her to balance. As far as the passive aggressive style is concerned, again, point out examples of this communication style in your everyday life. Help her see how, when someone uses this style of communication, the other person can often be left feeling confused, betrayed and disrespected.

The *Assertive* communication style is what we are striving for. Let her know that. An assertive communicator speaks with a firm tone of voice with great clarity and strength. Their thoughts take into account the needs of all the people in the conversation. Sadly, being assertive is sometimes confused with being "bossy," but they are very different. Help her notice her tone, and remind her to use her good leadership stance. Be clear and direct, but not mean or manipulative, and she will be on her way to getting what she needs.

A Golden Rule ... We want our girls and ourselves to use the *Assertive* style of communication 99% of the time. How do we do that you ask? Practice. You and her. Together.

Watch TED talks, or YouTube videos of women who are comfortable stating how they feel, what they think and what they want. People like Sheryl Sandberg, Amy Poehler, Emma Watson, Shonda Rhymes, Taylor Swift, Tina Fey, Oprah Winfrey, or Brene Brown, to name a few.

So many women aren't comfortable acting *Assertive* as they confuse it (and so do countless others) with acting *Aggressive*. They are very different styles. Think of being *Assertive* simply as direct and clear truth telling. It is always respectful, and as you can see from the grid above, both parties often "win" when you communicate *Assertively.* How can you feel bad about communicating when both parties win?

In my workshops, we do a great exercise I like to call "we're stuck." In this exercise, each parent in the parent/daughter pair puts the palm of their hand up against the daughter's palm. The two press their palms/hands against each other until I say, "Stop." I then ask the girls to push against their parent, and for the parent not to push back at all – and just notice what happens. I don't tell them anything else. When they are done, we debrief this game. Most often the girls expressed to me how much they loved trying to overpower their parents by pushing with great force. However, they noticed that when they pushed hard, their parents matched their level of pressure and pushed back. They got nowhere. I then ask the girls what they noticed about the game when their parents didn't push back at all. Nine times out of 10, my students will tell me that they stopped pushing so hard once the pressure on the other side let up, as there was no need to overpower them at that point.

"I didn't need to push when she wasn't pushing back," my student, Jordan, said. "It just felt easier to end the game."

BINGO! That's exactly what I want you and your girl to notice.

Realistically, if someone greets you with strong, negative behavior, then you are most likely going to match that person's level of pressure or force and push back. This is true in real life and online. However, if one of the parties involved lightens up the pressure, then most often everyone "lightens" up.

Girls encounter all kinds of communication styles in their relationships. Some are to be tolerated and let "slide," and some need to be addressed. Before your daughter can address a friend whose words or actions have caused her to feel a certain way, it's helpful for her (and you) to know the basics of what a true friend looks like. That way she can have a point of reference when thinking about what kind of behavior she can expect or is willing to tolerate. That will certainly guide the kind of conversation she initiates with that friend.

Friendship Recipe

As a fun exercise, sit down with you daughter and together create a list of characteristics that she appreciates in a friend. Suggest that she think of it as a recipe, like in cooking or baking, and show her the example below to get her creative juices flowing.

Note: Part of my *Social Media Survival Pack,* which you can access at the end of this book, will include a Friendship Recipe template that you and your daughter can customize.

Olivia's Friendship RECIPE

6 generous cups of love
1 barrel of laughs
5 tablespoons of adventures
3 large portions of loyalty
1 ladel full of listening
2 teaspoons of tears
4 heaping spoonfuls of honesty
1 can of kindness
unlimited amounts of hugs

Mix all together (along with a few squabbles that we
resolve together) and that's a true friend.

Now armed with her personal **Friendship Recipe** you can help her think more clearly about what a true friend looks like, and what kind of behaviors she can expect to see in a true friend. Help her understand that a friend can often have a bad day or make a mistake and treat her poorly (family can too). We might accept that person's apology and understand that they are learning. However, if a friend continues to display behavior that isn't in your recipe, it might be time to take a break.

An essential part of being able to communicate with others is being able to figure out how you feel. Not just on the outside, but on the inside, too. Knowing a broad range of words to use to describe how you feel can really help.

A Golden Rule ... All behavior is communication. We parents need to help our girls say how they feel and speak up. Next time you notice her behavior seeming "off," ask yourself (and maybe even her) a simple, "What really could be going on?"

At my workshops, we focus on teaching girls a broad emotional vocabulary. We break it down for the girls in a very easy to understand way. Armed with this book, so can you and your girl.

Identifying How You Feel

When we find ourselves having a feeling about a circumstance or conflict it brings up two types of feelings: External and Internal.

External Feelings are the first feelings that you most often feel in a circumstance. They are the feelings you can visibly see if you are walking by someone, and often are the easiest and fastest emotions to access. Some examples are annoyed or angry. They are emotions, but they don't really tell you that much about the circumstance, or how one could help make the situation better. They are non-descriptive and have a crudeness to them. They usually come to the surface faster.

X-RAY / X-TERNAL FEELINGS

X-TERNAL FEELINGS
(THE FIRST FEELINGS THAT YOU CAN SEE FROM THE OUTSIDE)
ANGRY
MAD
SAD
HAPPY

X-TERNAL BODY LANGUAGE
EYES LOOKING AWAY
ARMS CROSSED
PLAYING WITH HAIR
FIDGETING
SAYING THINGS LIKE "WHATEVER"

INSECURE
DISAPPOINTED
HUMILIATED
HURT
VULNERABLE
CONFUSED
ASHAMED
NERVOUS
PLEASED
REGRETFUL

X-RAY FEELINGS
(THE TRUE FEELINGS THAT YOU HAVE WHEN YOU LOOK VERY CLOSELY INSIDE TO FIGURE OUT HOW YOU REALLY ARE FEELING)

Internal Feelings are those feelings that you need to dig down deep into your belly and grab. They often require an imaginary x-ray machine to get a look at them. Internal feelings are vulnerable and special. Some examples of internal feelings are betrayed, anxious, embarrassed.

Just like an iceberg where only 10% of the whole mass can be seen above the surface, most people hide their true emotions below the surface. Only if we dig below the surface, and let those feelings come above, can others actually know and understand how we are feeling.

"Internal" feelings bring the truth to the surface. Thus if you share an "internal" feeling with someone, and it is not received as you would have liked, you will find that you still feel relief.

Relief for you have shared how you feel in a respectful manner, and have done your part.

Sometimes we falsely conclude what others are feeling based on our own assumptions. This doesn't serve anyone well. People can't know what we are feeling inside if we don't tell them. They are not mind readers. I know you know this, but it is easy to overlook when we are feeling strong emotions, or when we are on the receiving end of some. Therefore, in order to have someone change their behavior or help you, you must share with them how you are feeling. And the more specific you can be, the better able they are to change or help.

Now take a look at this chart below to get a sense of the many types of inside feelings there are. Hang this chart in your daughter's bedroom, or in a common area, and encourage everyone in the family to use these words when communicating. It will help everyone understand far better what is really going on when conflicts happen and emotions run high.

The idea is to start broadening the emotional vocabulary that everyone uses around your home. To get everyone in the groove with this idea, do some good role modeling and tell stories from your day. Then label the emotions that went along with the events that happened.

It's important to note that you will want to help your daughter think through who, where and when she shares her "X-Ray Feelings." Social media with its permanency, inability to elicit true emotions, and ease of access to "mock" someone behind their back is not an ideal place to share these "internal" feelings.

Note: Both of the above one sheets are part of your *Social Media Survival Pack* download.

Rose and Thorn

Another great way to practice labeling our "internal feelings" is by playing the game **Rose and Thorn**. In this game, you and your daughter each share with each other something wonderful and something not so wonderful that happened that day. The "rose" being the wonderful occurrence and the "thorn" being the not so wonderful experience. In your descriptions of your rose and your thorn, be sure to use good emotional vocabulary from your **How Do You Feel** chart. The more descriptive information you and your daughter can give about your roses and thorns, the better.

For example, a Rose from Mom:

"I felt proud when my Manager praised my creative analysis project at work."

A Thorn from Mom:

"I felt disappointed when my friend cancelled our dinner plans because she was too tired."

Now that you get the idea on how to help expand your daughter's emotional vocabulary, let's get her using it out in the real world, so she learns that by speaking up she can effect change in her own world.

The next step in this lesson is teaching your daughter how to use a basic "I" and "Can You" sequence, so that she can take how she feels and then plug it into a set of statements to simply express to someone both how she feels, and what she wants or needs them to do to make the situation better. We call the "I" statement the "moment of truth," as it's very important to be super-specific about how you feel, as well as what happened to create that feeling. No broad stroke judgments here. If you want scrambled eggs, ask the waiter for scrambled eggs. If you ask the waiter for just for eggs, he won't know what to serve you. The waiter needs specifics. So do the people on the receiving end of your conversations.

Hard Conversation Helper

Here is how it works.

I feel … (insert feeling emotion from chart here) *e.g. I feel disappointed.*

When you … (insert circumstance that occurred that made you feel the emotion you describe above) *e.g. When you don't invite me on your play date with Abby.*

Do you think you could … (insert what you would like them to do or not do anymore) *e.g. Do you think you could invite me sometimes?*

And I can … (what you could do to help the situation) *e.g. And I can try not to act jealous when you hang out with Abby without me.*

Easy-peasy, right?

It really can be.

Once you help your daughter identify what she is feeling and how she wants to change her situation, she will need your help to practice saying what she feels and needs (her "I Feel" and "Can You").

In addition, it's important to help your daughter learn how to enter and exit a difficult conversation with ease. Just like we discussed prior, if you start a difficult conversation in "attacking mode" and with "pushing behavior" then you darn well can expect that the person on the receiving end of the conversation is going to feel defensive and thus push back (remember the hands exercise where the parent/daughter were stuck as they both pushed on each other?). However, if you enter a challenging conversation by saying something positive about the person and/ or your relationship, right away you will disarm them. Together you can see the bigger picture which is that you care about each other and your friendship. And the same is true for ending a difficult conversation. No need to dwell on the issue that you just resolved or to make it awkward, think of something positive totally off topic and move along.

So we've:
1. Used our internal/x-ray feelings to explain how we are feeling.
2. Then we got really specific and explained exactly what the circumstance was that caused us to feel this way.
3. Then we asked for what we needed to make the situation better.
4. Lastly, we offered up something that we could do as well to make things better.

To help your daughter understand the importance of saying how she feels and asking for what she needs, you can tell her this story:

Jamie was afraid of the dark. She had been since she was a little girl. She will go on roller coasters, play with bugs, and walk home from school alone–but sleeping in the dark makes her uncomfortable. When Jamie slept at Scarlett's house for the first time and Scarlett's mom turned the bedroom and bathroom lights completely off, signaling it was time to sleep, Jamie felt scared. Really scared. Scarlett was talking and giggling in the dark, and having fun. Jamie was not. She was feeling very nervous, but was too embarrassed to say something.

Jamie had worked with me on communication skills, and knew that she had to say something despite her feeling embarrassed.

Eventually, Jamie shared with Scarlett how she was feeling.

"Scarlett, I feel afraid when you turn off the lights in the room."

"Do you think you could leave the bathroom light on, and I can try to be brave and adjust to the room being darker than what I'm used to at my home?"

And voila … the bathroom light was turned on.

Jamie was then at ease, and could join in on the giggling and fun.

She asked for what she needed and affected change in her situation.

Great story, right?

Ask your daughter what would have happened if Jamie had said nothing?

She would be lying there in the dark, scared, nervous and uncomfortable. Scarlett would have no idea of this, and not able to help Jamie feel more comfortable. Perhaps Jamie would make it through the sleepover, but would never sleep at Scarlett's house again, so she could avoid this happening again. Scarlett would feel hurt that Jamie never sleeps over, and their friendship would suffer because of it.

Jamie could have lost the friendship *and* had a terrible night's sleep, solely because she felt embarrassed to tell her friend her true feelings.

Our girls (and us adults) need to share what's going on under the surface of our icebergs. If we don't, others can't help us, and we lose sight of the truth that we can help ourselves.

Now these "I" and "Can You" statements are not magical fairy dust. It is important that both you and your girl know that. Quite often, she may handle her communication perfectly and still be met with external feelings and some push back from others.

That is okay. That does not mean they are not a friend worth keeping.

Sometimes others aren't ready to hear another person's true feelings, or they have never learned how to react appropriately when someone shares their feelings.

In that case, you can suggest to your girl that she dig further into her tool box of things to do in sticky situations and try something else.

Note: You may be feeling a bit overwhelmed by the "I" and "Can You" statements or any of the other communication skill learnings right about now. It's a lot. That's normal. You may never have been taught these things in this way before. Take it slow, and know that in my ***Raising Smart, Savvy, Self-Confident Girls in the #Selfie Generation*** program we really take these concepts off the page. I teach the program via video/webinar or individually depending on a clients needs. Plus, again, at the end of the book I provide a link for you to access my ***Social Media Survival Pack*** that contains the one sheet featured below called the **Hard Conversations Helper** which is a great tool to refer to with your girl.

HARD CONVERSATIONS HELPER

Ease The Negative Energy

Start your conversation with something positive that you like about your relationship so they don't feel attacked and know you care.

I Feel ...

Insert a feeling that you feel inside that needs an xray machine to find.

When You ...

Insert a very specific action that they took that didn't feel good.

Do You Think You Could ...

Insert what you would like the person to stop doing or start doing.

And I Can ...

Insert what you can do to make the situation better as well.

Okay Great ...

Once both parties agree to "do better" change the subject and move on immediately.

Not every "I" and "Can You" conversation is going to go perfectly. In fact, quite often, you may have to use different tools to move the situation along. Practice these tools as well with your daughter, so she gets comfortable using them.

Some other choices she can try are:

Walk Away. If the conversation isn't getting anywhere and she doesn't feel respected for having shared her feelings, then explain to her that it would be perfectly acceptable to simply move on and walk away. Politely and respectfully.

Ask The Toddler Why? Just like toddlers are always asking their parents, "Why?" Explain to your girl that she can do the same. Tell her to ask for more information from her friend. Maybe that will help her understand why the circumstance is as it is and help loosen things up.

True Friend Description. Your daughter can share with her friend how a "real" friend or family members should act towards each other. She can think about her friendship recipe and remind her friend what it means to be a true friend. She can provide some constructive feedback and help someone see a different way to interact.

Conflict resolution is a real skill. Encourage your daughter to practice scenarios with you or in the mirror so that when she is in the moment she will know what to say. If she becomes afraid of conflict, that's when we start to see those other, less effective communication styles pop up.

Note: Though these lessons are created for our girls, know that they are for us adults too, and can really help both of you with difficult conversations. Below is an even super easier way of managing a conflict with your own child whereby you both want something opposing.

Parent to Daughter 3 Step Conflict Resolution

This Hard Conversation Helper is super efficient. It goes like this:

"I know you ... (insert what the child wants in the situation)

"I want ... (insert what you want in the circumstance)

"How can we work this out?"

Then together you work it out, with you–as her parent and having had more experience–having the final say. This pays your daughter the respect that she needs as we discussed in Chapter 3 and goes a long way toward helping her develop critical thinking and negotiation skills.

Like we stated before, our girls want to feel heard. They don't want us to fix their problems. They want us to hold the anchor securely in place, so that they head back out into the sea to explore, and know they have a definite place to come home to. Teaching and role modeling assertive communication–where you share how you feel and ask for what you need–is a great way to do more of that.

Encourage your daughter to use these communication skills in person, or at the very least on the telephone. All of this great work gets lost in translation if it's done through a text, email or social media app.

She will surely push back when you suggest she could pick up the phone or talk to a friend during a break at school using these skills, but this is when you need to be the parent and stay firm on what you know is best. Refer to your family mission statement, or remind her about a rule in the social media usage agreement, the one that discusses taking time away from screens to have "in real life" socialization, and why both teach a valuable skill.

Lastly, share with her that real life is played out live, and in order to participate she needs to show up for the live performance. Hiding behind a screen just won't do.

Chapter 8

A MATTER OF PROPER MINDSET

Pssst, I know your secret. That's because it was my secret, too.

One of the reasons you are so darn scared of social media is because you don't want your daughter to mess up and have everyone around you see her mistake. Heaven forbid she be labeled "a mean girl" because she said something unkind on her Instagram account. What if word got out in your community that she posted something risqué, or even politically incorrect? Or how about the fear that she may overshare some personal information, or rant about the personal troubles of your family. It is enough to keep anyone up at night.

I get that.

In fact, many of the parents in my workshops expressed these feelings as well until we worked the **Thought Police** model and realized that being afraid of what "might" happen was getting in the way of our relationships with our daughters, our relationships within our community, and our relationship with ourselves.

So, I helped my clients change their thoughts around social media and their daughters…

From: "I worry that my daughter will see things on social media that make her feel badly about herself, and will not be comfortable speaking up or confronting people about how she feels when they say things that make her feel bad."

To: "I am getting comfortable with my daughter suffering small "hurts" and am teaching her the big picture values that are important in our family, and how she can reframe her thinking around what she sees online. I am modeling and teaching the communication skills she needs to be able to tell others how she feels, so that she can make change in her world."

...And their thoughts around others judging them.

From: "I worry that people will think I'm a bad parent because they see that my family is not perfect and that my daughter isn't perfect. I worry that they silently sit in judgment of our actions."

To: "Each day I try to be a better parent, spouse, friend and citizen of the real and digital world and understand that it's human to make mistakes. My daughter and I are doing the best we can right now."

So go ahead, do your own **Thought Police** work surrounding your fears. Try your best to stay conscious of the wayward thoughts that come into your mind, and with the help of this book, do your best to let go of that need to create the "perfect girl" or the "perfect childhood" for your daughter.

We are not striving for perfect here, people. Quite the opposite in fact.

You see, people don't care about you as much as you think. They're too busy thinking about what other people think about them. Now isn't that liberating?

I know, I know that's a pretty pessimistic thought. However, for many of my clients and girls this thought is freeing.

Truth is, not everyone is paying as close attention to what *you* are doing as you may think, or are afraid that they are. Armed with that knowledge, I suggest you and your daughter go ahead and do what feels right for you! Act as if nobody's watching because most likely they aren't.

On a similar note, we also know that not everyone is going to like us or include us in their lives or special events. And that's okay. Let's teach our girls to accept that and look at it through a different lens. Not one of exclusion and despair, but one of authenticity and strength.

A Golden Rule ... You will always be too much of something for someone: too big, too loud, too soft, too edgy. If you round out your edges, you lose your edge and what makes you unique. Apologize for mistakes. Apologize for unintentionally hurting someone. But don't apologize for being who you are.

Winston Churchill once said, "Success is the ability to go from one failure to another with no loss of enthusiasm." As a mentor and life coach, I express the importance for girls to flex their bravery muscles and try new things. We discuss how much pressure girls can feel to act perfect and be well liked, and we set the stage for them to understand that getting something "wrong" can often lead to more growth and strength than getting something "right" all the time.

Social media has brought on a confidence crisis of sorts. And it's playing out on two opposite fronts. Some girls are "oversharing" online, and looking for validation and connection when they are feeling their most vulnerable; other girls are "feeling frozen" and afraid to make mistakes, for fear of it being broadcast over social media to be seen and judged by all.

It's exactly those scenarios where we need to stand by our girls' sides. Quiet, strong and ready to support if they need us. Not ready to "fix" their efforts.

Just like we created leadership opportunities for our girls in our own homes in Chapter 5, we can create opportunities for our girls to stumble and then pick themselves back up.

Somewhere between that delicious baby girl smell and your need to protect your girl from the perils of "girlhood," you built a very tall fence around her to help keep her safe from falling. However, as you well know, it is those trees that have struggled against the harshest of elements and survived that can carry the heaviest load. When your daughter struggles, fails and then picks herself up and starts again – that is where the real growth happens.

Her spirit and belief in her own abilities forever strengthened.

Embrace A Growth Mindset

Just like in the **Root to Bloom: Creating Confidence** diagram, in order for our girls to experience the pride and joy of a "real accomplishment," they must experience struggle and even failure. Their confidence depends on it.

Carol Dweck's innovative research on the difference between fixed and growth mindset supports this notion.

In a *growth mindset*, people believe that their most basic abilities can be developed through dedication and hard work. That intelligence is malleable, not fixed, and if a student will focus on improvement instead of worrying about natural intelligence, they can learn more and get smarter. This view creates a love of learning and a resilience to setbacks that is essential for accomplishment.

In a *fixed mindset*, individuals dread failure because it is a negative statement on their basic abilities. In a *growth mindset*, individuals don't mind or fear failure as much because they realize their performance can be improved and that much learning comes from failure.

In these descriptions, you can clearly see the different way each mindset views the world and by extension, their own capabilities and opportunities for growth within it.

We need to start talking the language of a *growth mindset* with our girls. It's never too late. Praising their effort, not their results. Try believing, I mean really believing with every ounce of your being, that people do have the capacity to grow, learn, struggle and prevail.

Here's a great one sheet called, **Growth Mindset: What Can I Say to Myself,** that you can get in my **Social Media Survival Pack** and use to help shift your daughter and your language:

GROWTH MINDSET
WHAT CAN I SAY TO MYSELF?

INSTEAD OF...	TRY THINKING...
I am either good at it or not.	I can learn anything I want to.
My abilities determine my success.	My effort and positive attitude determine everything.
I am not good at this.	I am working to get better at this.
This is too hard.	This may take some time and effort.
If you succeed, I feel threatened.	If you succeed, I feel inspired.
I'm not good at math (or another subject)	I am going to work hard to grow my understanding of math.
I can't make this any better.	I can always improve; I'll keep trying.
Tell me I am smart.	Tell me I try hard.
I feel embarrassed, I made a mistake.	Mistakes help me improve and learn.
I'll never be as smart as my friend.	I am going to figure out how she does it so I can try it too.
This is good enough.	Is this really my best work?
Plan "A" didn't work out.	Good thing the alphabet has 25 other letters since Plan A didn't work out.

When you change your approach to praise, you're changing the achievement marker from a value judgment on the inherent intelligence of your daughter, to a series of messages throughout your child's life that places value on the process of learning.

It means a child's self-worth and confidence in trying things for the first time doesn't become tied to how well they can immediately perform, or how inherently smart they are –which provides welcome relief for them. Quite often, this shift is what is responsible for enabling them to achieve what they set out to achieve, because they know they have more than one chance to prove themselves.

This isn't just the latest parenting trend. Through research, Carol Dweck has begun proving that a *growth mindset* can make a significant difference. She tracked a group of kids who entered their school year with almost identical test scores, and noted which kids displayed *growth mindset* attitudes at the beginning and which ones held the beliefs of a *fixed mindset*.

"We measured their mindsets – we saw whether they believed intelligence was fixed or could be developed. ... They had entered seventh grade with just about identical achievement test scores. But by the end of the first term, their grades jumped apart and continued to diverge over the next two years. The only thing that differed were their mindsets. They had completely different goals in school. The number one goal for kids in the fixed mindset is 'look smart at all times and at all costs.' So their whole lives are oriented toward avoiding tasks that might show a deficiency. But in a growth mindset, where they believe intelligence can be developed, their cardinal rule is 'learn at all times and at all costs.'"

Dweck goes as far as to argue that the growth mindset will allow a person to live a less stressful and more successful life.

Learn To Fail ... To Learn

We adults have gotten so busy protecting our girls from the perils of social media, being left out, bad grades and other transient disappointments that we have lost sight of that through failure and struggle we create within them the belief that they have the ability to bounce back and be in charge of their lives.

They need to believe this to feel confident. They need to experience this first hand to believe it. In their bones, in their soul and in their being.

We're building confidence from the inside out, here.

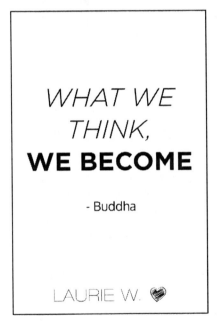

WHAT WE
THINK,
WE BECOME

- Buddha

LAURIE W.

So parents, I beg of you, resist dropping off your daughter's lunch, her forgotten school books, or controlling what she wears (so long as it's not objectively inappropriate) for fear of the consequences and ridicule.

These minor humiliations and punishments will build character and put the power of life choice back where it belongs: in her own hands, where it should be more and more as she grows.

To gain confidence, the girls need to feel capable and competent. Slowly ramping up to handling their own daily stuff as they grow older will help them to feel this way.

Please know that when I suggest to do something I never mean or expect it to be 100%. We're all just trying our best. My goal is just to point out some of the bigger picture thinking at play here. By all means if your daughter forgets her lunch or school work one day, and you are available to help, go ahead and drop it off and be sure to stick a **Positive Post** in with it.

Remember, you are just the gardener tending to the beautiful flowers. Your job is only to help the young flower be able to flourish on its own eventually.

We have an acute, almost biological impulse to provide for our children, to give them everything they want and need, to protect them from dangers and discomforts both large and small. And yet we all know – on some level, at least – that what kids need more than anything is a little hardship and some challenges that they can overcome, even if just to prove to themselves that they can.

However, it's one thing to try out failure in the privacy of our own home or small community, it's quite another to have it play out in public splashed all over social media for the world to see. (And possibly never be deleted!)

That's hard, but we can't allow it to hold us back. Too much is at stake. We have to stand strong knowing that with rules in place, and with you by her side, she will prevail. She can make and survive her mistakes.

Bravery takes skills and practice. One is not born brave vs. a coward. Like confidence, some people are born with an innate ease with which they take risks, however being brave is a skill one can learn. And it doesn't have to look like that Hollywood moment when you do something amazing, bravery is about small triumphs.

And bravery needs compassion.

So often when someone messes up others say, "It's okay, you will be fine." But what they could say that would feel really helpful would be, "Wow, that really stank huh? So glad you are ok. Just know this happens to others as well."

No false promises or pushing her through what she is feeling, saving her from her feelings or denying her that disappointment.

Countless leaders past and present say that the experiences that enabled them to achieve the success that they have, were not built in their years at private schools or Ivy League colleges, but they came out of their taking chances and living without a safety net. Trial and error bring about real accomplishment and that enables growth.

I am hoping that at this point in the book, you have seen the benefits of allowing your daughter and yourself to make mistakes, and to also let go of the wayward thoughts that don't serve you.

I told you in the beginning of this book and I will say it again.

You. Are. Not. In. Control.

Embrace this idea. You never were, and never will be, in full control.

And as you can see from the tenets laid out in this book, trying to be in control may be ruining your own life as well as your relationship with your daughter.

Life is messy, mysterious and magical. So hold onto the golden scepter as you stand by your girl's side and watch her bloom.

Chapter 9

POSITIVE INTENTIONS AND MAKING SPACE FOR CHANGE

The one thing most studies on happiness agree on is this: Family and relationships are the surest way to happiness.

Close behind are meaningful work, positive thinking, and the ability to forgive.

What does not seem to make people happy are money, material possessions, intelligence, education or attractiveness.

Did you know that the happiest countries in the world are in the bottom half in terms of wealth, and in the U.S., once you get above $70k in annual household income, there is absolutely no statistically significant effect of more money on an individual's daily wellbeing.

I bet you intuitively knew that.

As we near the end of this book, I want to offer you one last tool to use to help connect you with your daughter, yourself and the Universe. I have created a *Gratitude and Power of Positive Intentions* class for kids and I am excited to share the basic tenets of it with you, so that you can begin to bring it into your home.

Gratitude and Power of Positive Intentions

Here are the basic principles:

Be aware of the vibrations "vibes" that you are putting out into the world.

Your vibration consists of your attitudes and beliefs about the world in which you live. Your vibration is the energy you are putting into the Universe, be it positive or negative. Focus on the lack in your life, and you will get more lack. Focus on abundance and you will bring forth more abundance.

Always strive to put forth good energy and positive "vibes."

Positive energy attracts things that you want. This is why the happy-go-lucky people you know seem to flow through life effortlessly, and why people who are already financially secure continue to attract more opportunities and money as they are operating from a worldview that focuses on abundance.

Believe you can bring what you want into your life through these basic principles:

1. Identify what you *do not* want. (Don't focus your thoughts here.)
2. Get clear on what you *do* want. (Start focusing your thoughts here.)
3. Feel what it would be like to have those things that you want in place.

For example, if you want greater success in your career, Then do things that will have you feeling "successful" as a byproduct and start focusing your attention there. Maybe it's running a fulfilling community service project or playing in a tennis tournament, whatever you choose, know that when you bring that feeling that you are after into your life (success and accomplishment in this example) you set things into motion to bring forth more of it.

Allow positive things to happen in your life.

Adopt an open, "absence of doubt" attitude. Believe that things will work out, let go of trying to control the outcomes and watch the magic begin to happen.

Show gratitude.

Showing gratitude is very powerful. When you show that you are grateful for things that you have in your life, it helps attract even more things for you to be grateful about. Quite simply, when you are grateful you attract most effectively.

Kids aren't born with thoughts. They develop them over time from what they hear from adults. Kids can feel our fears, doubts and prejudices. Their default thoughts and vibrations are often shaped by us, the adults who care for them. Kids hear us worrying about money, doubting that good things will happen, getting scared that we may lose our jobs, and faking a smile after telling them, "It's all okay," even though we hardly believe that's true. They pick up our negative emotions like sponges. If they sense we're scared, they get scared. If we worry about having enough money, they worry about having enough money. And it becomes their default vibration in addition to the script in their thought playbook. It's often unconscious as they grow into adulthood, but those attitudes and fears will follow them, the same way some have followed us from our childhood. That is why we need to pay close attention to the energy that we put forth in our homes.

So if you're often thinking, "I'm lame," then your energy is lame—and you attract lame and disappointing experiences into your life. The opposite experience occurs when you think high-level thoughts like, "I am awesome!" When you think and feel "awesome" you exude an energy of confidence. In turn you will find yourself attracting exciting and eventful experiences into your life. Each thought you have informs your energy, and then your energy manifests into your experiences. Your thoughts and energy create your reality.

Work to teach your daughter to direct her thoughts, beliefs, and expectations in a positive way so that she can learn to bring the things she really wants from life. Kids who learn about Gratitude and The Power of Positive Intentions, learn to be positive people who dream big and have great success in life. A little bit of effort to teach these principles today will pay off in dividends for your daughter down the road.

Here are some easy and fun things you can do to bring **The Power of Positive Intentions** into your family life:

1. **Teach your child to set intentions.** Big or small. Literal and figurative. Intentions simply bring awareness to what we are doing. It gives us a chance to pause, reflect and be an active participant in our own experience. It's easy to spend our lives in reactionary mode, but with a planned intention — an idea formed in the heart — we can help our daughters and ourselves experience our days as we want (or intend). For example, in the morning, help your daughter choose how she wants to feel throughout her day; joyful, at ease, happy! Then help her set her intention. Talk about her day ahead and discuss possible things that may "come up" to derail her from feeling joy, happiness or at ease. Ask her to picture, in her mind, handling whatever situations may come up that could keep her from feeling happiness and ease.

2. **Play The Appreciation Game.** Gratitude is one of the highest vibrations in which we can live. Our feelings of gratitude attract into our life more of those things that we will appreciate. At mealtime or bedtime, or even while driving carpool, ask your daughter to think of one or two things she

is grateful for. Teach her that as she expresses gratitude, more things will show up in her life for which she can feel grateful. Magic!

3. **Create a Personal Vision Board or Family Wish Box.** Visualization and creating consistent reminders of one's intentions are key in helping attract what you want into your life. So how about creating a personal vision board? Have your daughter cut out images of what she wants and then paste it onto a board. A puppy, a pair of sunglasses, to make the soccer team, a vacation in Mexico. Another way to do this is to create a Family Wish Box, and have her place images and/or representations of what she and other family members want in the box. The key is that the images or representations must feel really good to everyone. It could contain details of things you want to do together, or things you want as a family like a new car. Put the board or box in a place where everyone in the family can see it. Talk frequently about how much fun you will have, or how much you will enjoy these things once you have them. Even pretend you have already had the experience, and talk about how great it was. I know it seems silly–but acting as if it has already transpired really helps attract that thing to eventually happen. It's a great activity and connects her dreams and wishes together.

Note: The Wish Box is a great place for her to put all those things that she sees on Instagram and asks you if she can have; experiences too. Help her think through her desires, and begin to create her life consciously. When parents and children both fully realize that they have an innate power to attract, amazing things begin to happen.

Making Space for Change

"So what now?"

You're feeling inspired and ready to make some changes in your home. You're excited to create your own family mission statement, and ready to clean up some of those old childhood wounds that keep reappearing.

Well, now starts the hard part...because as we already established, you are not in control.

Your daughter may very well not be interested in having more rules surrounding social media usage at home.

Your partner may not want to change his own media consumption habits, or do all the fun, connected family time things I've laid out in this book.

Your friends and extended family may tell you that you are crazy and to just "let it go" or have their own advice to offer, which may or may not be right for your family or won't sit well with you.

You may find yourself right back in the throes of "busyness" and feeling overwhelmed. *Too overwhelmed* to create the change you want.

It's going to be hard. I am not going to sugar coat it for you.

No, it's not rocket science or brain surgery, but it is change. And change is hard.

But life does not get better by chance, it gets better by change.

So I am going to ask you one final time. Perhaps it will be the most important time in our whole time spent together. Don't pay attention to any of those obstacles that lie ahead of you. Don't find reasons this journey will be hard or anticipate the resistance that hasn't even happened as of now. Go ahead and grab that darn golden scepter and seize the power.

Don't let the obstacles that lie ahead hold you back from creating the family life you desire. Don't let resistance from others keep you small, and certainly don't let it prevent you from building a better version of you – right now.

Your daughter needs you to step up ... now! (please)

Because if you don't, that darn uninvited guest, Social Media, is going to ravage your whole house. (No Tate's cookies, Stacy's chips, Haribo gummy candies or kale salad to be found anywhere.)

Common Sense media tells us that 1 out of every 2 teens feels addicted to her mobile device.

78% of teens check their devices at least hourly.

77% of parents feel their teens get distracted by devices and don't pay attention when they are together, and 41% of teens feel their parents get distracted and don't pay attention.

Both parents and child agree that mobile use is both distracting and a regular source of conflict.

Yes, school is a pressure cooker, and social media is "stealing her soul," as some of my clients have complained. It is affecting her focus, her social wellbeing, and is creating a hostile environment in your home.

We as parents must take a central role in mitigating the effects of social media and the pressures our daughters are feeling both in real life and in their "alternative universe." We need to be the buffer of the culture, and help our girls remain grounded in a value system that is true to themselves.

I care about you.

I care about your daughter more.

Let's help her grow into the brilliant flower that she is destined to become.

This is not going to be easy.

There is not one way to execute this plan. That's why it's important for you to find someone to partner with on this undertaking. Maybe it's your spouse or a family friend who shares your value system, or perhaps you will decide to join my program called, ***Raising Smart, Savvy, Self-Confident Girls in the #Selfie Generation.*** Whatever you decide is right for you, just make sure you have a plan and cheerleaders around you. If you don't, you will get stuck in the weeds. I don't want to see you get stuck in the weeds. You have a garden to bloom.

Chapter 10

THOUGHTS ON WHAT YOUR DAUGHTER ISN'T SAYING

"Sometimes, could you tell me your opinion in just three words?"

What she's saying is, less is more. You don't always have to have a "Hallmark™ moment" with her to get your point across.

"Act approachable. Otherwise, I'll keep my stories to myself"

Kids, like horses, can feel your energy before you say anything. If you're tense, nervous, focused on getting that email out, they know – and will stay away.

"Think before you react. Would you want to be treated this way? If not, then don't treat me that way either."

Sometimes, when you're in the heat of the moment, you may say something that will do more harm than help. Ask yourself before you say something critical, "Would I treat my friend like this?" If the answer is no, then certainly don't treat your daughter that way.

"Sometimes, just sometimes, it would be nice if you could point out when I'm doing something right instead of wrong."

Every once in a while, catch your girl doing something good and let her know you appreciate her. Just because.

"Say 'yes' more than you say 'no.' The world is going to give me lots of 'no's' as I get older so could you give me a few yeses until then?"

Life is an adventure. Instill in your daughter a sense of wonder that she can do anything she wants – all she has to do is try (and ask your permission of course).

"When I come home, could you stop looking at your smart phone, move away from the computer and stop talking to your friend? Pay attention to me, even if I don't speak. I'll be gone before you know it."

We parents must stay conscious and aware of how available we really are to our girls when they are in our presence. Must. Save your computer "errands" for a time when she is not home.

"I know what you think of me. I'm a mind reader. So think nice things!"

So often in our quest to help build a better "me," we focus on the things that our daughter is doing wrong so that we can "fix" everything. What we really should be doing is focusing on the *good* things. Put your focus there, and watch her sparkle.

"You are right. You don't have to say something 10 million times for me to finally hear you, you have to say it 10-million-and-one times."

Parenthood is like the ultimate marathon: long, grueling, exhilarating, but worth the pain and effort in the end. So yes, you do have to say the same things over and over sometimes, because you never know just when that moment will arrive when you see it "click." Instruction often requires more repetition than you think before knowledge is automatic.

"I do value family time. I just don't want to value it all the time."

What teenagers want most of all are social rewards, especially the respect of their peers. Becoming an adult means leaving the world of your parents, and starting to make your way toward the future. A future that they will share with those peers. So enjoy your time with your daughter. Make family time fun, and let her enjoy her friend time, too. Try and include her friends in some family activities to increase the strength of all of her ties.

"Don't spoil me. I know that it's not good for me to have it all. I'm only testing you."

In these busy times, it's so easy to fall into the habit of giving our girls extra money for lunch, or to order in dinner with friends, or to buy another pair of this or that. Sometimes, it seems like a small indulgence or an easy way to assuage our own guilt when we are busy. However, we are not doing anyone a favor by doing this. The real world will not be handing her 20's just because she asked.

"Don't correct me in front of people. I will pay closer attention if you do it in private."

You are on your girl's home team. In fact, you're her best (and only dedicated) cheerleader, so why would you ever want to humiliate her in front of others? Plus, who can actually hear a "life lesson" if they are too busy feeling ashamed?

"When I am feeling out of control, yell and push you away, do the opposite. Stay right where you are. Hold the line."

You are family. You are her parents. She is supposed to give you her worst. And you are supposed to be her rock. Her anchor. Just stay close and steady for her. Show her that this too shall pass, and you'll be right there when it does.

"Don't make me feel badly when I make a mistake. It puts too much pressure on me. I can't be perfect."

Our girls just want to be girls. Sometimes, they want to leave the food pantry messy to go back out to play, and admit they forgot their homework assignment at school without us making such a big deal out of it. Sure we've got big picture lessons to teach about responsibility, but sometimes that can wait 'til later. Not every mistake signals a crisis or needs intervention.

"Follow through on your consequences. Others will, so help me learn that now."

We are trying to teach our girls to be leaders. Part of that entails teaching them how to make good decisions, and that every decision has a consequence associated with it. Skip the consequence part of the equation, and the whole lesson is lost. See it through.

"Don't promise things you know very well you can't keep. I get easily let down."

It's so easy to casually suggest to your girl that over the weekend you two will go to the mall to look for a new outfit for her upcoming party, or out for Frappuccinos. Then life happens, and the outing just doesn't occur. Your intentions are good, however sometimes your follow-through is lackluster. Try to avoid making promises you are not sure you can keep. Not only will you be role modeling more honest communication, but it also will take away the little "hurts" she experiences each time the plan changes.

"Don't tell me my fears are silly. They feel very real to me."

We want our girls to share their feelings with us so we can help them bring about change in their situations. Even though you may have plenty of life experience to put certain fears and ideas in perspective, these are very real to your daughter and it may have taken a lot of courage for her to voice them to you.

"Don't put me off when I ask questions. If you do, I'll stop asking and find the answers elsewhere."

Enough said. I know you are worried about where else she is getting advice, otherwise you probably wouldn't have bought my book. She needs to know that all of her questions are safe with you, and that guiding her from a place of love is important to you.

"Don't think that you can't apologize to me. Nothing makes me feel better then to know that you make mistakes, too. Show me how to handle that and put the relationship first."

Showing your daughter that you are human and make mistakes too is one of the best things you can do to build her resiliency. And, showing your daughter what it looks like to be genuinely sorry and make amends is developing a crucial life skill.

"Don't pretend you are perfect."

Your daughter doesn't want to have to be perfect, and neither do you. It's way too hard to keep that up. So how about you let it go … for good!

"Don't be mean to your body in front of me."

Our girls are paying very close attention to how we treat and talk to our bodies. Very close attention. Those patterns of behavior are hard habits to break, but it's imperative that you realize you are the primary role model for your daughter on body image. Try and make sure she knows what it looks like when one is at peace with her body and food. Even if you have to fake it (a little, or a lot).

"Eat dessert."

Your daughter wants to enjoy the sweetness of life and she wants you to come along for the ride with her. Why not indulge a little bit on occasion? Plus, it helps her learn moderation to see that you can sometimes have "your cake and eat it too!"

"Don't question my honesty all the time. I can easily frighten, and even start telling lies to stop you from getting involved."

I know we want to teach our girls the value of being honest, but how we approach the sensitive topic is crucial. Tread lightly.

"Don't take too much notice of my small ailments. Sometimes they get me the attention I need in that moment. I'll be fine."

All behavior is communication. So when your daughter is hurt and just wants a little extra TLC, well, then give her that TLC. The ailment is secondary. Being there with her in the moment, quite often, is what she is truly after. (Unless there is a lot of blood, of course. But I am sure you've already covered family first aid – that was part of those easy preschool and elementary years, right?)

"Don't let it upset you if I say mean things. It isn't you I hate, but I resent when I feel you use your power to thwart me."

Growing up isn't easy. You remember that, right? Our girls are going to act out, say mean things, make mistakes and tell white lies. Accept it, and let your girl know that there's nothing she can do that would change how you feel about her (okay, maybe not *nothing*, but you get the idea). Tell her you "love her, even though (you) don't love her behavior." It's a great go-to reminder when you want to pull your hair out, trust me.

"Don't be afraid to be firm with me. I prefer it. Makes me feel more secure."

Girls need rules and boundaries to bump up against. It makes them feel safe. It shows them you care. Better yet, engage her in a two-way conversation about these rules, and you'll be showing her firsthand the art of communication, negotiation and collaboration. Perhaps, you will even be inspiring the way she raises her own daughter

"Labels are for jars, not people. Stop using them. It confuses me."

Role model the behavior you want to see. Don't pollute your daughter's mind with labels or blanket statements about people, things and ways of being. Let her discover her own thoughts, and enjoy the world for as long as she can through her curious, open eyes.

"Sometimes just zippy your lippy and let it slide ... "

As our daughters get older, more and more, they simply want and need us to listen and be there for them. No judgments, no life lessons. Just be there.

Chapter 11

Marching Orders

My wish for you is to have the courage and staying power to put these ideas into action.

I wish that you will stop looking around for the answers and grab the golden scepter you already possess and reclaim the joy in your home.

Rules, boundaries, shared family traditions and leadership lessons are a great place to start.

You got this.

I could have written a 500-page book with even more client stories, and exercises for you to worksheet your way through, but I know you are busy and have work to do. I wanted to set you on your path *right now.*

So let's get going ...

First, go ahead and grab my ***Social Media Survival Pack*** by visiting https://www.lauriewolk.com/social-media-survival -pack/

The Social Media Survival Pack Contains:
- Social Media 101 (cheat sheets)
- Family Media Agreement(s)
- Think B4 U Post (one sheet)
- House diagram (a reminder to keep those doors and windows mostly closed)

- Root to Bloom: Creating Confidence (one sheet)
- Family Mission Statement (template(s) to create your own)
- Friendship Recipe (template(s) to create your own)
- Social Media: Hurt, Harm, Handle It (one sheet)
- Communication Styles (one sheet)
- Hard Conversation Helper (one sheet)
- Positive Posts (template to create your own)
- "How Do You Feel" diagram (one sheet)
- Growth Mindset: What Can I Say to Myself (one sheet)
- Thought Police (one sheet)
- Power of Positive Intentions (one sheet)
- Share our Stories "Fill in the Blanks" Journal for Parent and Child to Write in.

Take some time to look over the materials and refer back to the sections of the book in which it was covered. Jot down the notes that will help you when engaging the other family members, whether it be your spouse, your daughter, or even your own parents or siblings.

Then pick a date and a time when you feel ready to start putting some of the items in this book into action. Decide what is the first item you want to tackle. Start the discussion about your own Family Media Agreement, or perhaps you want to do something fun first, and create a custom Family Mission Statement.

Whatever you choose to do, first give yourself some "snaps," because that is progress. *We're looking for progress, not perfection.*

If you know that you want to put many of these concepts into action but don't know if you will truly do it without being held accountable, then visit my website, lauriewolk.com, for more resources and to learn about personal coaching..

Either way, I am here for you. I will cheer you on and hold the space for you as you help your daughter bloom to her full potential. Join me in an intimate group online or do it yourself, the power is within you. If you want help, guidance, or a community to belong to while you take on this work, come find me at LaurieWolk.com and schedule a free consultation to see if I can help you and your daughter on your journey.

An Open Letter to Our Daughters

Dear Daughter,

Hi! My name is Laurie W, and I am the author of *Girls Just Want to Have Likes: How to Raise Confident Daughters in the Face of Social Media Madness.* Someone who loves you, perhaps a parent, just finished reading my book, which means they are interested in finding new and fun ways for your family to connect, and to help you grow into the amazing young woman you are destined to become.

The point of my letter is two-fold. First, to introduce myself. Hello ☺! Second, to share with you the ideas that are covered in my book, so that you also understand the concepts behind things that you may start to notice happening in your home life. Like more "fun" family time, the opportunity for you to get more involved in doing things (like organizing family vacations) that can help you develop important leadership skills. There will also be some *mutually agreed upon* rules surrounding social media in your family.

In my book, I explain to your parents that texting, social media, video chatting and streaming videos are an important part of your life. That they are tools you use to connect with your friends and provide an important relief for you from your busy life, which is jam packed with school work and after school activities.

A little bit about me: I am a social media expert and mentor, and I teach leadership, social skills and communication to girls of all ages. I help parents and girls learn how to connect with each other, identify how they feel, and ask for what they need. This is especially important in today's world, with so many young women like yourself spending time on their smart phones and other "screens" instead of talking "in real life" to one another. Have no fear though, I am not suggesting that you ditch your smart phone, no way! I love social media and I really love pop culture. In fact, before becoming a girls' leadership coach, I worked at E! Online, as an expert in those areas. What is so great about my perspective, which informs my book, is that I get it. I am on both sides: yours, and your parents' as well. I am here to help both of you communicate better, understand each other's feelings, and have more fun. The #1 goal of the book is to help *you* become the best person that you can be, and to have fun while doing it.

At I believe that leadership starts with a small letter "l" and not a big capital L. Our goal is to help you learn how to lead *yourself* first and foremost. To speak up in class, recognize what a "true" friend is, and share with them how you feel without fearing losing the friendship. I want you to risk making a mistake, knowing that you will learn more from failing something than from succeeding. I know, hard to believe – but true.

Here are the chapters in the book and a quick description of what they discuss so you too will be up to speed on how to help you sparkle like the star you are.

Boundaries: As discussed above, in this chapter I teach your parents some basics of social media and help them understand that it provides necessary downtime for you. However, access to social media and screens 24/7 is not good for anyone. We all live "in the real world," so it's important that, together with your parents, you set up some rules surrounding digital media usage. These should cover basics on how to be a good digital citizen, such as "If you don't have anything nice to say, don't post it at all." On my website, I have a media usage agreement that you can go through with your parents and choose which rules and lessons could best apply to you. The goal is for you to have a two-way conversation with your parents surrounding social media. With this in place, you can hopefully move on to having more fun together, and you will stop hearing, "Put down your phone!"

Family: No one can make you as mad as your own family members, right? And nobody is going to love you unconditionally as much as your family. In this chapter, I offer lots of engaging ways in which you can bring the fun back into your family. We know that your adolescent years are filled with friends and fun after-school activities. Sometimes, family seems less exciting. However, we also know that spending time connecting with your family, and building a strong foundation from what your family believes in, is going to help you immeasurably as you continue to grow up.

Leadership Skills: Here, I offer your parents some easy and fun ways in which they can create opportunities for you to use leadership skills in your day-to-day life. Things like planning the family dinner, creating its shopping list, preparation and cooking (with help at first). It also means teaching and encouraging you to speak up in class and in front of others when you find the opportunity.

Healing & Role Modeling. You are going to love this section, as it turns the camera on your parents. I challenge them to take a look at their own behavior, past and present, and how their personal experiences may impact the things they might be saying to you as their daughter. Everyone can use some rules surrounding technology, and I ask your parent(s) to become more aware of where and when they are using it; For example, how often are they on *their* phones or computers when you are together? Do they ever text and drive? (Yikes!) How about other life lessons that they are trying to teach you, but not really doing those things themselves? Like being brave about trying new experiences.

We all need reminders on how to be our best selves, no matter what age we are. However, when you work together as a team and support each other without judgment, it is much easier to notice and then change your behavior. Parents are not perfect, and that is a good thing. That helps you to realize that *you* don't need to be perfect, either.

Communication Skills: If you are anything like me, sometimes you text or comment on social media as a way to easily engage in conversation but not have to fully "deal" with the emotional commitment of "real life" socializing. I get that. And it totally works in many circumstances. However, I know you will agree that we all live "in the real world" and need to know how to have difficult, embarrassing and even scary conversations with people face to face. This section of the book gives your parents some words, phrases and ideas which they can use to model the skills and behavior involved in helping you work out touchy stuff. This will help you feel comfortable being brave and having difficult conversations when they come up in real life. Like in sports or playing an instrument, you get better at things with practice. Practice communicating with people how you feel, and what you want from them, and you will see that this skill will develop in no time. Just like juggling. Okay fine, maybe not juggling – but you get the idea.

Mistakes and Growth Mindset. In this chapter, I discuss how important it is for your parents to show you that they make mistakes, and that it's okay for you to do the same. We also discuss how important it is for everyone in the family to think of things in your life as being able to grow and change with time. Like a flower; not a fixed rock. For example, math may be hard for you now, but you can work to get more comfortable with math. It is not already decided that you will be "bad" at math forever just because you struggle with it currently in school. Some things will come more easily to you, but you can always grow, learn and try different approaches to the things that both interest and challenge you. You are not a rock! Great leaders all agree that it is the mistakes that they made, not the successes they achieved, that have made them the smartest and strongest. I understand how hard and embarrassing it can be to make a mistake, especially if it's broadcast on social media, in class or on the playground for all to see. Trust me on this one, nothing truly helps you develop your strength, courage and can-do attitude more than having failed at something. Knowing that you can make a mistake, even a bad one, and still survive will show you that all can surely be okay again no matter what happens.

Positive Thinking. This chapter is an important part of bringing more happiness and ease into your family's life. The concept is that if you get very clear about what it is that you want more of in your life, and stop focusing on those things that you don't want or are afraid of, you will be happier. By taking a positive approach, and knowing what you are looking for, you will potentially attract those things that you want into your life. For example, if you focus on how scared you are of big crowds, avoid going to big concerts or games, read news stories about bad things happening in large crowds, you will confirm to yourself that this is a fear worth believing. Focus on the fun that you want to have at the concert or ball game, and the feeling of being safe and having a good time with lots of like-minded people, and you are more likely to feel that way. This is not magic fairy dust and doesn't work all the time, but it is helpful in teaching your brain how to think about those things that you *do* want in your life and giving less attention to those things that you *do not* want. When you focus on the wrong things, then those undesired things sometimes come into your life.

Well my new friend – can I call you my friend? That's pretty much it. I hope you learned that not all adults are opposed to social media – and that together with your parents and loved ones, you will learn about and even implement some of the things described above. Even if you focus on just one thing – for example, more family outings – that's amazing.

My dream for you is that you love and appreciate yourself and that people treat you with love and kindness, and you do the same in return. I want you feel comfortable speaking up and being brave. I know it's not easy, but know that there are lots of people there to support you on your journey to becoming a fully bloomed flower.

Now go get 'em!

Love and Learning,
Laurie

P.S. To start you on your way to really connecting and appreciating each other, I have created a fun Journal for you to fill out with a parent, sibling or grandparent. My hope is that this will help you learn something new about your parent(s) or loved one and see that your family really is pretty fun and interesting.
You can access it here: https://www.lauriewolk.com/ejournal/

ACKNOWLEDGMENTS

Well hello there. I know you usually skip over the acknowledgements page but in this case would you mind taking a look-see. I want you to know all the wonderful people who helped me get to where I am today; A published author.

Bulah - None of this would be possible without you. You are brilliant in every way. You jumped right in and took over while I went ahead and wrote the book that has been inside me for so long. When you say, "Whatever makes you happy honey," you actually mean it and that means everything. You are the salt to my pepper, the yin to my yang, and the mustard to my ketchup. Our family's lives are funnier and sunnier because of you. Scarsdale meets Ho Beach, a perfect combo!

J - Your bravery and resilience astound me. The complexity of your being continuously pushes me to strive to be the best person I can be. You showcase building confidence from the inside out brilliantly and bring such greatness into the world with your infinite creativity, compassion for all living beings and irresistible sassiness. Your willingness to try new things and pick yourself up if they don't go as planned is inspiring. I am privileged to call you my daughter. Oh and put down your iPhone, please, I am paying you a compliment here. Geez!

R - You are a gentleman through and through. Always teaching lessons that even us adults still need to learn. It takes my breath away every time I see you from afar and realize that you are fast approaching manhood; capable, compassionate and oh so handsome. The world has infinite possibilities for you. Remain true to who you are, let go of perfectionism and believe in yourself. Happiness is yours for the taking and I can't wait to watch you fly. P.S. Would you mind cooking up something delicious before you head out flying?

S - The light within you shines so bright that I find myself smiling from ear to ear from the warmth of your glow. You are the perfect blend of silly and sentimental and I am blessed to call you my daughter. I cherish every day that I get to witness the beautiful young woman that you are becoming. You have taught me so much about how to just be yourself; brave and bold, competitive, and compassionate. Oh and thanks for allowing me to cuddle, read and make videos with you late into the night. Keep doing you S, It's pretty darn awesome. "We are going to a Party!"

Revis, my pup, thank you for the warm kisses and for staying up late with me while I wrote and everyone else was peacefully asleep. I promise I will start posting your handsomeness on Instagram again soon.

Mom - Your Unconditional love and always-listening ears are my forever "home." You have no idea how beautiful you are both inside and outside and therein lies your true beauty. Continue to step into your greatness and take risks as you forge this new life stage. I love you to the moon and back a zillion times.

Dad – Without even quite realizing it, you helped me find my own voice as a strong, capable woman. Your intellect, curiosity and innate sense of honor inspire me to do good in the world.

Extended Family and Besties - Thanks for standing by my side and believing in me even when I didn't always know where I was headed. And thanks for allowing (and responding) to my million texts and emails asking for advice on whatever the "thing" of the day was. And to my "jeweler," I never had a sister but if I did, I would want her to be just like you. Your perspective on everything always clears my focus. Nothing better than sharing the ups and downs with the "family" you choose.

My Gaggle of Girlfriends - You are my role models, my comedy relief and my inspiration. You each are a force to reckon with in your own right and bring such unique things into the world and to our friendship. In gratitude.

Morgan James and My Book Launch Team - Indeed it takes a village. Grateful for all the inspiring advice, comedic banter and support.

Girls Leadership – Thank you for allowing me the privilege to represent such an amazing organization doing so much good in the world.

And for the people who said "you'll never write a book" …

Nanny nanny poo poo.

And finally, a big thank you to you for reading my work, attending my workshops, classes and being open to new things. You, (yeah you), really matter!

ABOUT THE AUTHOR

 "We all have a Wonder Woman inside us."

Laurie has always enjoyed empowering others. A "go to" girl since childhood and a cheerleader at heart, she loves to help people become their best selves. Her passion is helping parents and young girls learn how to communicate and connect with themselves, each other and the outside world.

Through mentoring, coaching and leading workshops, she works directly with parents and young girls on building confidence, leadership and digital citizenship skills. Laurie's goal: teaching girls how to put down their phones and develop "in real life" communication and relationship skills. Laurie works to reach this goal through writing curriculum, speaking engagements, workshops, one-on-one guidance and leadership programs. Just as she encourages girls to do, she uses her knowledge and influence to inspire others — both online and in the real world.

A graduate of Emory University, Laurie received her Bachelor of Arts Degree in Psychology. She received advanced certification at the Martha Beck and Girls Leadership Institutes. She is on the Board of Girls Leadership and the Westchester Children's Museum.

An engaged and hands-on mother of three, Laurie has been called a "modern mentor" as she understands kids and connects with them both as a guide and a friend, teaching them important social and emotional skills that will serve them for a lifetime.

Laurie can be found at Lauriewolk.com and Laurie@lauriewolk.com

THANK YOU

Social Media Survival Pack

This isn't the end but rather the beginning. Exclusively for readers of *Girls Just Want to Have Likes: How to Raise Confident Girls in the Face of Social Media Madness,* there is a free download available that offers readers many of the lessons and tools mentioned in the book,

Download the Survival Pack here: https://www.lauriewolk.com/social-media-survival-pack/

Fun and Interactive eJournal for You and Your Girl

In addition, Laurie has created a **eJournal** for you and your daughter to fill out and use as a fun way to connect and get to know each other's hopes, dreams and secrets. Download eJournal here: https://www.lauriewolk.com/ejournal/Parenting Program: Raising Smart, Savvy, Self Confident Girls in the #Selfie Generation

Exclusively for readers, Laurie is offering a discount on her **Raising Smart, Savvy, Self Confident Girls in the #Selfie Generation** program. A perfect way to create accountability and dimensionalize many of the concepts laid out in the book. Email Laurie to receive your discount code at Laurie@Lauriewolk.com

Let's Keep Talking

Laurie is available for one-on-one coaching, groups, online webinars, corporate conferences, curriculum development and "brown bag" lunch talks. Visit LaurieWolk. com or email her at Laurie@lauriewolk.com to start the conversation about having Laurie as a speaker at your event, on your podcast, radio or television program.

If you enjoyed this book, one way to express your gratitude is to write a review on Amazon so others can find *Girls Just Want to Have Likes* as well.

Doing Good Feels Good

Part of the income from this book will be donated to My Sisters' Place of Westchester, New York. My Sisters' Place provides confidential shelter, programs, education and advocacy for battered women and their children.

LAURIE LOVES READING

Blessing of a Skinned Knee, Wendy Vogel, Ph.D.
http://www.amazon.com/Blessing-Skinned-Knee-Teachings-Self-Reliant/
dp/1416593063
Brainstorm: The Power and Purpose of the Teenage Brain, Daniel J. Siegel MD.
http://www.amazon.com/Brainstorm-Power-Purpose-Teenage-Brain/
dp/0399168834/ref=asap_bc? ie=UTF8
The Curse of the Good Girl, Rachel Simmons http://www.amazon.com/
Curse-Good-Girl-Authentic-Confidence/dp/014311798X/ref=sr_1_1?s=-
books&ie=UTF8&qid=1463266827&sr=1-1&keywords=curse+of+the+good+girl
Queen Bees and Wannabees, Rosalind Wiseman http://www.amazon.
com/Queen-Bees-Wannabes-Boyfriends-Realities/dp/0307454444/
ref=sr_1_1? s=books&ie=UTF8&qid=1463266863&sr=1-1&key-
words=queen+bees+and+wannabees
American Girls: Social Media and the Secret Lives of Teenagers, Nancy Jo Sales.
http://www.amazon.com/American-Girls-Social-Secret-Teenagers/dp/0385353928/
ref=sr_1_1? s=books&ie=UTF8&qid=1463266938&sr=1-1&keywords=ameri-
can+girls+social+media+and+the+secret+lives+of+teenagers
Untangled: Guiding Teen Girls Through the Seven Transitions into Adulthood,
Lisa Damour
http://www.amazon.com/Untangled-Guiding-Teenage-Transitions-Adulthood/
dp/0553393057/ref=pd_sim_14_2? ie=UTF8&dpID=5lo4hqwNSHL&d-
pSrc=sims&preST=_AC_UL320_SR212%2C320_&refRID=0AQXENCB-
1HQRAZ383PYZ
Self-Coaching 101 by Brooke Castillo http://thelifecoachschool.com/wp-content/
uploads/2012/03/Self-Coach-101-eBook.pdf
"The Problem of Rich Kids," Suniya S. Luthar, Ph. D.
https://www.psychologytoday.com/articles/201310/the-problem-rich-kids

"How Successful Leaders Spent Their Teenage Years," By Auren Hoffman http://
time.com/3859359/leadership-teenage-years/
"The Letter Your Teenager Can't Write You," Anonymous
http://www.bluntmoms.com/letter-teenager-cant-write/
"Cool at 13, Adrift at 23," Jan Hoffman
http://well.blogs.nytimes.com/2014/06/23/cool-at-13-adrift-at-23/

Morgan James
Speakers Group

We connect Morgan James published
authors with live and online events
and audiences whom will benefit
from their expertise.

CPSIA information can be obtained
at www.ICGtesting.com
Printed in the USA
LVOW12s1630220817
545953LV00005B/908/P